icons of
rock
JOHN LENNON

icons of
rock
JOHN LENNON

Terry Burrows

Brown
PARTWORKS

ISBN 1 84044 066 X

Produced by **Brown Partworks Ltd**
8 Chapel Place, Rivington Street, London EC2A 3DQ, UK
www.brownpartworks.co.uk

Managing Editor: Lindsey Lowe
Project Editor: Rob Dimery
Design: Wilson Design Associates
Picture Manager: Susannah Jayes
Production Manager: Matt Weyland

Picture Credits
Archive Photos: 58. **Associated Press:** 90. **Camera Press:** Elena Dair 162.
Corbis: 20, 54, 102, 172; Bettmann 98, 108, 142, 144, 146, 148; Brojan Brecli 119;
UPI 44, 80, 94, 96, 118, 170. **Hulton-Getty:** 8, 10, 15, 16, 18, 24, 30, 34, 38, 43, 46, 48, 50,
56, 68, 70, 71, 74, 82, 84, 88, 110, 121, 136, 140; Apple Corps Ltd 62, 64, 78, 100. **London
Features International:** 150, 152, 164. **Mirror Syndication:** 114. **Pictorial Press:** 12, 32,
40, 42, 60, 92, 122, 124. **Popperfoto:** 52, 67, 86, 87, 168. **Redferns:** 72; Tom Hanley 13,
106, 134; K&K Studios 23; Astrid Kirchherr 25; Jürgen Vollmer 158. **Retna:** 14; Jak Kilby
116; David McGough 166; David Putland 174. **Rex Features:** 22, 36, 65, 76, 95, 104, 156;
Stephen Morley 138, 157. **Topham:** 112, 154.

Front cover: **Hulton-Getty**
Back cover: **Corbis-Bettmann**
Title page: **Rex Features**

Printed and bound in Italy

Contents

Introduction

Late on December 8, 1980, news of an earth-shattering event filtered across the airwaves of the world. John Lennon, one quarter of the most famous pop group the world has ever known, was dead. Aged 40, he was murdered by a fan outside his New York home. The chilling broadcasts were hard for many to comprehend. John Lennon was loved and respected the world over—and now a shaken world mourned its loss.

Lennon was not just a popular musician. By the end of the 1960s he had also become one of the most prominent standard bearers for world peace—even if his methods did not always meet with the wholehearted approval of the Establishment. Accompanied and inspired by his partner, controversial performance artist Yoko Ono, Lennon instigated a series of protests and publicity-grabbing events to put the issue of peace on the world's front pages.

John Lennon was born in a maternity ward during a lull in the fierce bombing of Liverpool by Germany's Luftwaffe in World War II. His early childhood followed a traumatic path until he was adopted and brought up by his mother's sister, known to him throughout his life as Aunt Mimi. From a young age John's comic writing, witty artworks, and sharp tongue marked him out as an independent thinker. However, he singularly failed to channel his undoubted intelligence into schoolwork, becoming ever more disruptive and troublesome to his teachers. In his mid-teens, like so many others of his era, John found a new and exciting means of salvation from the terminal boredom of the classroom—rock and roll. When the music of the first great wave of American rock stars, such as Elvis Presley, Little Richard, and Fats Domino, made it across the Atlantic he was instantly and completely captivated.

In an age when pop and rock music has long lost its ability to shock, it can be difficult to appreciate the impact that the musical revolution of the mid-1950s had on disaffected youngsters such as John Lennon. Before rock and roll, teenage culture barely existed—you were a child until you left school, at which point you abruptly became an adult. But with rock and roll, teenagers finally had a style of music they could call their own. It was widely condemned by the adult world, and as a result, the generation gap was born.

Although Britain spawned a handful of its own rock-and-roll stars, they were largely inferior copies of the real thing. Of greater interest to John Lennon was the "skiffle" fad, spearheaded by Lonnie Donegan. Skiffle showed that anyone with a guitar and the patience to learn three chords could get up on stage and do their thing—a principle that would re-emerge 20 years later with punk rock. John was ripe for the calling, and quickly formed his own school skiffle group, called The Quarrymen.

By all accounts a shambolic unit, John's band played wherever and whenever they could find a gig. It may all have been fun, but The Quarrymen were heading nowhere until a momentous event took place on Saturday, July 6, 1957, when they played at a local village fete. The band's performance that day was inauspicious, but this time they were watched intently from the side of the stage by another young skiffle fan. After the show, John's friend Ivan Vaughan introduced him to this fellow aficionado—a 15-year-old called Paul McCartney. History was now in the making.

In December 1962 "Love Me Do," The Beatles' debut single, entered the national charts. Hearing them for the first time, people presumed they were a new group. Most people were unaware of their trips to Hamburg, their seven-hour stints on stage in the nightclubs on the Reeperbahn. Stints that had turned The Beatles from an ordinary group of teenage musicians into a tight-knit combo. No one who heard them had any idea of how they would affect popular culture during the next seven years. Their music apart, the world was completely unaware that everything connected with the group—their hairstyles, their suits, and their attitudes—would define the new decade. Right up to their miserable demise in 1970, the fortunes and activities of The Beatles' camp mirrored the path of an entire decade. For many—and that includes some of us who were too young to know about it at the time (or had not even been born)—the 1960s remain such special years because they were touched by the genius of The Beatles, and especially that of John Lennon.

Although it's well over a quarter of a century since they made their final recordings, The Beatles remain the most famous pop group of them all; their classic recordings increase in stature with the passing of time. John Lennon's later solo recordings didn't always shape up to the impeccable standards of the Fab Four, but songs such as "Imagine" remain consistently popular. What's more, Lennon's uncompromising stance continues to inspire many successive generations of young musicians. That he is one of the great icons of rock music is now taken as read. In future years there can be little doubt that John Lennon will be remembered simply as one of the twentieth century's most significant icons.

1 The Early Years

Born in 1940, during a lull in the German bombing of Liverpool, John Lennon's early years are traumatic. He is a smart child, but school can offer no useful outlet for his talents. His vivid imagination is only truly captured by one thing: rock and roll. From the age of 16 he channels all his energy into his school band, The Quarrymen. Six long years later, The Quarrymen have transformed themselves into The Beatles. They learn their craft playing long sets in the clubs of Hamburg's seedy Reeperbahn district. When they return to Liverpool, they are ready to take on the world.

War baby

The city of Liverpool was not the safest of places to live in Britain during the early days of World War II. As one of England's major points of embarkation to America, the naval shipyards and miles of commercial dockland along the River Mersey made it a particularly valuable target for the Luftwaffe—Nazi Germany's airforce—which was by then making regular bombing sorties over mainland Britain.

During the summer of 1940 Liverpool had been devastated by a series of night raids, although the first week of October had seen an unexpected lull in enemy activities. German hostilities, however, were the last thing on the mind of young Julia Lennon as she lay in Liverpool's Oxford Street Maternity Home preparing for the arrival of her first child. Late in the afternoon of October 9, Julia went into labor and at 6:30 p.m. she gave birth to a son. In a fit of patriotic fervor she named him John Winston Lennon, after the country's wartime prime minister, Winston Churchill.

Julia had been born in 1914, one of five daughters. Her father, George Stanley, was employed by the Glasgow and Liverpool Salvage Company, a firm that thrived during World War I—the Mersey's geographical importance meant that no expense was spared in the effort to clear blockages in the river resulting from mounting shipwreck debris. The steady work made the Stanleys slightly wealthier than most other "Scousers" (natives of Liverpool).

Julia was the least conventional family member. She met her future husband—a ship's steward named Freddy Lennon—in Liverpool's Sefton Park. Julia made fun of a hat he was wearing; to make her laugh, he sent it skipping across a lake. Much to her family's dismay, the pair became an item, and eventually married in December 1938. However, theirs was not to be the closest of relationships. Freddy worked on the great passenger liners that journeyed between Liverpool and New York City, and the couple routinely spent months apart.

When war broke out in September 1939, Freddy's liner was berthed in New York; he evidently wanted no part in the war, for he promptly jumped ship. As a result he was arrested, and the maintenance checks that he had been sending to Julia ceased—the couple's marriage soon fell apart as a result. Freddy returned to Liverpool for a few brief conjugal visits but these became increasingly rare. Something of a "ne'er-do-well," he eventually ended up serving a sentence for desertion at a British military prison in North Africa. He returned a couple of times—once in 1940 and again in 1942—before disappearing from Julia and John's life, apparently for good. It was only when John became famous as a Beatle that his father emerged from obscurity.

Wartime Liverpool. Due to its importance as one of England's most strategically valuable dockyards, the city was devastated by the Luftwaffe's bombing raids.

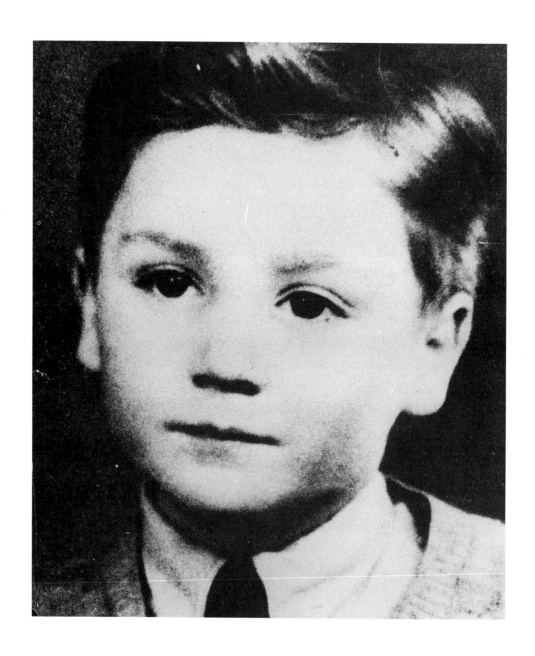

Aunt Mimi

Wartime was especially tough for young single mothers, whose numbers steadily increased as the war progressed. Julia became unsettled; the footloose and fancy-free times she had enjoyed before the war began to seem a lifetime away. And now she had the added responsibility of looking after young John. The burden of childcare often fell on the rest of her family. It was clear that her elder sister Mary Elizabeth—known to the family as Mimi—was forming a close relationship with John. Although happily married, Mimi and her husband George Smith had no children of their own, and she doted on Julia's son.

After the Allied victory in the Battle of Britain during 1941, the Luftwaffe bombings became rarer and life in Liverpool slowly began to return to normal. Julia was still young and attractive and soon had a new man in her life.

She was working at a café in Penny Lane when she met a waiter named John Dykins, and quickly decided to move in with him. Julia saw her life with Dykins as a new beginning, a chance to start a new life. However, the problem remained of what to do with her son; Dykins did not want the responsibility of bringing up another man's child.

Although Julia's refusal to face her maternal responsibilities angered her family, a satisfactory solution soon became clear: John would be adopted by Aunt Mimi. Thus it was that at the age of nearly five John Lennon went to live with his aunt and uncle at "Mendips," a semidetached house at 251 Menlove Avenue, Woolton—a pleasant middle-class suburb three miles outside of Liverpool's city center. From that moment onward, Mimi took her responsibilities as John's guardian very seriously indeed, forging a close, loving relationship with him that would last for the rest of his life.

John Lennon's artistic leanings were self-evident from an early age. He was a bright boy and could read by the age of four. His education started at Dovedale Primary School, near Penny Lane. Mimi would drop John off every morning and pick him up at the end of the school day at a bus stop by Penny Lane roundabout. One of John's earliest interests were the "Just William" stories, which were widely popular at the time. Richmal Crompton's tales of a disruptive 11-year-old boy appealed to young John's sensibilities. John also excelled in art at Dovedale and soon began writing and drawing his own books and comics. He also began to develop a taste for the petty mischief that would get him into trouble time and time again in the future.

Opposite: Dovedale Primary School pupil, John Winston Lennon.

Right: John's Aunt Mimi, who raised him from a young age.

Young teenage rebels

In September 1952, when he was 12 years old, John was sent to Quarry Bank High School, a traditional English grammar school that could boast a distinguished record of academic success. John started at the school with high hopes and good grades. However, with his friend Pete Shotton there to aid and abet him, his academic performance soon started to suffer. As Shotton remembers, "We started in our first year at the top and gradually sank together into the sub-basement." Lennon and Shotton soon found themselves in the company of Quarry Bank's least distinguished pupils, close to the bottom of "C" stream. By the age of 14, the pair had become notoriously disruptive troublemakers and detention became a weekly event for them. Mimi came to dread the periodic phone calls from the school secretary telling her of John's latest misdemeanor.

Although John loved Mimi, his mother had always remained in close contact with him and visited most weeks. As he grew older he began to see more and more of her, often playing truant to do so. John treated Julia more as an older sister than as his mother. For her part, Julia always encouraged John to have fun rather than worry about the future, and his irreverent sense of humor clearly stemmed from her.

When the American phenomenon of rock and roll hit Great Britain during the mid-1950s, John's life was changed forever. The most fervent fans of this new music were the notorious "Teddy Boys," young rebels who wore outlandish draped jackets, frilled shirts, and skintight "drainpipe" trousers; their greased locks formed quiffs, known as "DAs," which flopped down over their foreheads. John loved the music, the look and the sense of rebellion that rock and roll provided. Along with thousands of other young British teenagers, he fell under the spell of the U.S. rock and rollers, especially Elvis Presley. He nagged at Mimi and Julia to buy him rock-and-roll clothes and records, and set about turning himself into a teenage Teddy Boy.

The British scene had its own rock-related fad—skiffle, which was popularized by ex-jazz musician Lonnie Donegan, who covered American folk songs by the likes of Woody Guthrie and Huddie Ledbetter. Based around the simple sound of an acoustic guitar and/or banjo, a stand-up double bass (or a homemade equivalent, fashioned from a pole, a string, and an old tea chest), and a washboard rhythm, skiffle groups sprang up overnight all over the U.K. And John Winston Lennon was not going to be left out of the new craze.

Opposite: John, the teenage rocker.

Right: Lonnie Donegan, the leading light of the skiffle trend that swept through the U.K. during the early and mid-1950s.

The Quarrymen

From the moment he first heard Lonnie Donegan launching into the million-selling "Rock Island Line," John became fixated with the idea of getting a guitar. Even the frugal Mimi eventually had to give in to his persistent demands. One Saturday morning, she accompanied John down to Hessy's music store in the center of Liverpool and paid 17 pounds (approximately $25) for a cheap, steel-string acoustic guitar. She had a warning for him, though: "The guitar's all very well, John, but you'll never make a living out of it."

Her words fell on deaf ears. With all the enthusiasm that they'd failed to put into their schoolwork, Quarry Bank's resident teenage rebels, Lennon and Shotton, formed their own skiffle group—The Quarrymen. John sang and played the guitar while Pete played along on the washboard. They were joined by a variable assortment of skiffle enthusiasts that at one point included schoolfriends Nigel Whalley and Ivan Vaughan on "tea-chest" bass, Rod Davis on the banjo, guitarist Eric Griffiths, and drummer Colin Hanton.

Like many other teenage skiffle groups, The Quarrymen performed Lonnie Donegan's songs alongside American rock-and-roll hits such as "Blue Suede Shoes." The Quarrymen started to get engagements at school dances and youth clubs, though they rarely brought the house down. In fact, it was only John's enthusiasm that kept the band going—most of the others were only doing it for a laugh. But John had found something that he could give himself to heart and soul. He would often strum his guitar so hard that he would break a string; when this happened, he would borrow Rod Davis's banjo and play that while Rod set about trying to fix the string.

On July 6, 1957, The Quarrymen were booked to play at St. Peter's Parish annual church fete in Woolton. They were due to perform on the back of a lorry during the parade, and then afterward on stage at the fete itself. The event turned out to be highly significant—not only for John Lennon, but for the future of pop music.

Ivan Vaughan, no longer playing with The Quarrymen, turned up at the fete with a schoolfriend from the neighboring Liverpool Institute. Ivan was keen for John to meet his friend—he felt sure that they had a lot in common. So, as The Quarrymen played their set that day, Ivan's young friend Paul McCartney watched intently from the side of the stage. Afterward, Paul met up with the group backstage in the Church Hall and ran through the Eddie Cochran classic "Twenty Flight Rock" as well as a few Little Richard numbers. A mildly inebriated John Lennon assiduously studied Paul's guitar-playing skills.

The Quarrymen at the Woolton Village Fete, July 6, 1957. Left to right: Eric Griffiths, Colin Hanton (seated in the background), Rod Davis, John Lennon, Pete Shotton, and Len Garry. Paul McCartney watched their set that day from the side of the stage.

The Fab Three

The first meeting between John and Paul was a shy and awkward one in which little was said. However, though he might not have shown it at the time, John was very impressed by Ivan Vaughan's friend. Paul McCartney could not only tune a guitar, he also knew a wide selection of chords; John was still limited to playing variations on the banjo chords that Julia had taught him. Paul had also learned the words to numerous rock-and-roll hits by heart; John had recently taken to making up his own lyrics, principally because he could never remember the real ones all the way through.

The arrival of Paul presented John with a problem. The Quarrymen had been an extension of his school gangs, in which he had obviously been the leader. Paul was remarkably self-assured, and John realized that he wouldn't be able to boss him around as easily as his other friends. At the same time, Paul was simply too good not to be in the band. It is difficult to imagine two more different personalities—John, rebellious with his dry wit always ready to issue a sharp put-down, and Paul, ambitious and hardworking, with a desire to please everyone around him. Nevertheless, despite their differences, the two quickly became friends.

By the late 1950s, the face of pop music had changed once more. Electric guitars were now taking over from the acoustic instruments favored by skiffle bands. Paul and John also became aware that rising stars from across the Atlantic, such as Eddie Cochran and Buddy Holly, were writing their own songs. (Previously, singers had mostly relied on professional songwriters to provide them with material.) This inspired a highly competitive period that saw John and Paul each writing new songs as if their lives depended on it.

Around the same time, Paul had struck up an uneasy friendship with a fellow pupil at the Liverpool Institute. Young George Harrison, who was already a talented guitarist, soon began hanging around at Quarrymen gigs. George was only 14 years old at the time and when Paul suggested letting him join the band, John was horrified. But when he heard George play, and when the youngster told The Quarrymen that they could rehearse at his parents' house, John began to change his mind. Before long, George was in.

From the moment The Quarrymen first spluttered into life, John's fate was sealed. First skiffle and then rock and roll became his new teachers, and his schoolwork deteriorated sharply as a result. However, the arrival of a sympathetic new headmaster at Quarry Bank, William Pobjoy, temporarily extended John's academic future. Pobjoy realized that the only subject John had any interest in was art. He therefore used his connections to arrange a place for the teenager at Liverpool College of Art, where John duly arrived in September 1957.

Even at the age of 12, George Harrison was a gifted guitarist. Less than three years after this photograph was taken he joined The Quarrymen.

Art school

Although English art schools have nurtured many of rock's big names, including Pete Townshend of The Who and The Kinks' Ray Davies, John found the experience a sobering one. He'd been a hopeless pupil at Quarry Bank, but he'd been popular with his classmates and his anarchic behavior earned him a certain kind of respect. But Liverpool College of Art seemed to him to be filled with goatee-bearded jazz fans. And they weren't too impressed by the Teddy Boy in their midst. "When I was at art school they'd only allow jazz to be played," John later recalled, "so we had to con them into letting us have rock and roll on the record player by calling it 'blues.'"

John struck up an unlikely friendship with another "outcast" student at the college. Stuart "Stu" Sutcliffe was an outstanding young artist—one of his tutors claimed he was the most talented artist the college had ever produced. Moreover, he possessed a markedly intense personality and an unorthodox dress sense—skintight jeans, pointed boots, and brightly colored shirts—that was more outrageous than John's by far. He also adopted a pair of dark glasses that, along with his swept-back hair, gave him a strong resemblance to James Dean. Stu's unconventional dress sense aroused suspicion among his fellow students, but his obvious talent forced the college authorities to turn a blind eye to his appearance. John and Stu quickly became close friends.

Drawn by Stu's unique outlook and sheer coolness, John decided that he had to have him in his band. There was a problem, however: Stu had never played an instrument and showed no evidence of musical ability. But John's persistence paid off. One of Stu's paintings had been selected for the biennial John Moores Exhibition in Liverpool, a considerable achievement. It was bought by John Moores himself, for the princely sum of 65 pounds. Stu went to Hessy's music store with the money and bought a Hofner "President" bass guitar.

Paul McCartney could see why John would want someone like Stu in the band, but had misgivings about the new bassist. McCartney was talented and ambitious and felt that Stu's lack of musical ability would hold the band back. During much of Stu's time with the band, John would feel compelled to protect him from Paul's carping.

On July 15, 1958, John's world was turned upside down. Following a visit to Mimi's house, his mother Julia was knocked down and killed in a road accident. John was devastated. Julia had been a carefree spirit who had always indulged his moods and attitudes and her death haunted him for much of his life. John later dedicated many songs to his mother, and named his first son, Julian, after her. Paul McCartney had lost his mother as a teenager, and the shared experience rapidly brought the two closer together.

John's close friend Stuart Sutcliffe—talented artist, flamboyant dresser, and early Beatles bassist.

Germany calling

Progress was slow. The Quarrymen needed a drummer and regular work. In 1959 they entered a talent competition in Manchester as Johnny and the Moondogs, but met with no success. Then, early in 1960, the band contacted local promoter Alan Williams to see if they could get gigs supporting the U.S. stars who played at the Empire, one of Liverpool's main venues. Williams was not that impressed by The Quarrymen, but did offer advice and occasional work. When he told them to get a new name, "something like The Crickets," Stu jokingly suggested The Beetles, after Marlon Brando's biker gang in the 1954 film *The Wild One*. John's adaptation—The Beatles, a pun on the "Beat music" that Liverpool's bands played—was initially rejected. They settled on The Silver Beetles.

Above: John the rocker in Hamburg, 1960.

The band's first break came when they were asked to back minor English rock and roller Johnny Gentle on a short tour of Scotland. They returned to find that Williams now had a lucrative deal with German strip-club owner Bruno Koschmider, and was sending local groups to play at Koschmider's clubs in Hamburg. One band dropped out in July 1960 and Williams offered the job to The Silver Beetles, who promptly recruited a drummer—Pete Best, whom they met at a Liverpool venue called the Casbah Coffee Club, run by Best's mother. And by the time they reached Hamburg, the band had settled on The Beatles. John finally got his way.

Their first residency was at the tiny Indra club, in the middle of Hamburg's notorious red-light district, the Reeperbahn. The Beatles' home for the next two months was a seedy room at the back of a cinema also owned by Herr Koschmider. The workload was heavy. Sets often lasted for several hours and the band usually played more than one set per day. Permanently exhausted, their employers gave them amphetamine pills ("speed") to pep them up. During the first month, The Beatles honed their stage act and often slipped original Lennon/McCartney songs into their set. The arduous schedule made them a tight and powerful rock-and-roll band, and they were soon promoted to play at Koschmider's larger Kaiserkeller club.

However, disaster struck in November 1960. A routine police inspection revealed that, at the age of only 17, George Harrison was too young to be playing in a nightclub after midnight. He was immediately deported. Days later, McCartney and Best were arrested, allegedly for trying to burn down Koschmider's cinema, and were also deported.

Opposite: The band formerly known as The Silver Beetles in Hamburg, 1960. Left to right: Stu Sutcliffe, John Lennon, an unknown friend, George Harrison, Paul McCartney, and Pete Best.

The Cavern

The Beatles had gone to Hamburg with high hopes, but their dramatic premature return left them feeling dejected. Stu was hit the hardest. While in Hamburg he had fallen in love with a young photographer, Astrid Kirchherr, who had taken a number of striking photos of the group during their stay. It was Astrid who influenced The Beatles to comb their hair forward in the style favored by her German student friends. This was to give rise to the famous Beatle "mop top" haircut.

On their return, The Beatles discovered that Liverpool's beat scene had developed, creating its own style and sound. They also found that they now had something of a reputation as a live powerhouse in Liverpool, spread by other "Merseybeat" bands who had visited Hamburg and seen them play. The Beatles had left Liverpool as a bunch of no-hopers and returned as one of the city's hottest acts.

At the heart of the Merseybeat scene was The Cavern jazz club in Mathew Street, and at the end of January 1961, The Beatles began a legendary residency there. They were paid 25 shillings per day for two 45-minute sets—easy money for a band used to playing nonstop for five hours. Their set featured covers of often obscure American rock-and-roll and rhythm-and-blues hits, brought across the Atlantic by merchant seaman—one of the reasons why Liverpool's musicians often got to hear new music before anyone else in Europe. It was at The Cavern that teenage girls first started to scream at The Beatles. And initially, the object of most of the female attention was drummer Pete Best.

In April 1961, The Beatles returned to Hamburg's Top Ten club, but while the band seemed to be going from strength to strength, internal pressures between Paul McCartney and Stuart Sutcliffe were growing. Over the weeks that followed, Stu gradually eased himself out of the band, ostensibly to study at Hamburg State Art College under Eduardo Paolozzi, one of his idols. He was to play no further part in The Beatles' story. Tragically, Stu died a year later from a brain hemorrhage, just days before The Beatles were due to play at the Star Club, a major new rock venue in Hamburg. Astrid told The Beatles of Stu's death when she met them at Hamburg airport. John was devastated, though his initial, shocking reaction was to laugh hysterically. "It was his way of not wanting to face the truth," Astrid explained later.

Above: John photographed by Astrid in her Hamburg loft.

Opposite: John at The Cavern, clad in Hamburg leathers and playing his first Rickenbacker guitar.

Under new management

By the middle of 1961, rock and roll was such big business in Liverpool that the city had its own music paper—*Mersey Beat*—and several stores that specialized in selling beat music. The city's best record store was NEMS (North End Road Music Stores), an electrical retail outlet that boasted the "The Finest Record Selection in the North." The store was part of a chain run by the Epsteins, a wealthy Jewish family. The record department had been built up successfully by the owner's son Brian, a 27-year-old former drama student.

Brian Epstein was proud to claim that he was able to obtain any out-of-stock records his customers wanted. He was therefore somewhat annoyed when, on October 28, 1961, a teenager named Raymond Jones came into the store to ask for The Beatles' recording of "My Bonnie." Epstein had heard of neither the group nor their record. In fact, the song had been recorded in Germany by a singer called Tony Sheridan, who had used The Beatles as his backing group on the session. (At the time it was only available in Germany and was credited to Tony Sheridan and The Beat Brothers.) A couple of days later, two girls came in to ask for the same record. When one of Epstein's customers told him that The Beatles were a local group who regularly performed at The Cavern, he felt compelled to investigate further and on November 9, accompanied by his assistant Alistair Taylor, he headed down to the club.

The sweaty, noisy atmosphere of a Cavern lunchtime session was a new experience for Brian Epstein, but he was immediately struck by the power of The Beatles' music and their sense of humor on stage. Epstein returned to The Cavern several times to watch the group and gradually an idea began to form in his mind. Seeing the effect The Beatles were having on The Cavern's lunchtime crowds, Epstein could see no reason why this phenomenon should be limited to Liverpool. In early December 1961, he asked the band if they'd like him to be their manager, and on December 15, they signed a management contract with him. Although he agreed to play no part in their musical direction, Epstein henceforth took control of every other aspect of the band's day-to-day existence.

His first task was obvious enough. As far as the Merseybeat bands were concerned, The Beatles were now at the top of the pile. But outside the area—even just up the road in Manchester—they were more or less unknown. Brian Epstein knew that the only way of promoting The Beatles was to bring them to the attention of the big London record companies. Getting his band an audition wouldn't be difficult: as the manager of one of the biggest record stockists in the north of England, no label would want to risk upsetting Brian Epstein unnecessarily. As far as he was concerned, The Beatles' music would do the talking.

Brian Epstein, The Beatles' suave but fragile manager. In the background is London's Saville Theatre, which Epstein leased in the mid-1960s as a venue to showcase his acts.

Meeting George Martin

The first label Epstein approached was Decca, one of the most powerful record companies in the U.K., who arranged an audition with the group for January 1, 1962. In the space of three hours, The Beatles recorded 15 tracks. The band was not really satisfied with the performance, but Epstein was convinced it would be enough to secure a deal. However, Decca felt otherwise, rejecting The Beatles because they sounded "too much like The Shadows." Dick Rowe, the head of artists and repertory at Decca, told Brian Epstein that guitar bands were on the way out, a rebuff that John and Paul referred to in a later interview:

Paul: He must be kicking himself now.
John: I hope he kicks himself to death.

While Epstein was furious at Decca's rejection of The Beatles, the band itself was more sanguine: "Don't worry Brian, we'll have to sign to Embassy," John wisecracked. (Embassy was an albums-only label owned by the Woolworth's chain that released out-of-date, low-quality LPs that sold for the price of a single.)

The band's fortune soon changed, however. Epstein hit on the idea of using the Decca audition tapes to make a demonstration disc to play to prospective labels. He paid a visit to the famous HMV store on London's Oxford Street, where it was possible to have one-off records cut from a master tape. The engineer who processed the record took a liking to The Beatles' sound and suggested that Epstein take it to EMI's publishing wing. That same day, Epstein visited EMI's head of publishing, Sid Coleman, who listened to the record and also liked what he heard. He agreed to publish two of the songs—the Lennon/McCartney compositions "Love Of The Loved" and "Hello Little Girl." Furthermore, Coleman agreed to set up a meeting with George Martin, an EMI talent scout and producer.

George Martin was unusual in the pop field in that he'd had classical music training, and had studied at London's Guildhall School of Music. He'd also worked with Spike Milligan and Peter Sellers, two of The Goons—stars of a legendary British radio show of the 1950s. But as rock and roll was the record industry's biggest money-spinner, Martin had reluctantly begun looking for talent among the countless newly formed beat groups. It was with few expectations that he sat down to listen to the latest demo tape to come his way. On the evidence he heard, The Beatles seemed to have little to distinguish them from many other well-rehearsed groups. But he was sufficiently interested to offer them an audition. As he later recalled, "I thought to myself: 'There might just be something there.'"

An impressed George Martin hears a run-through of an early Beatles song at Abbey Road Studios.

Meeting George Martin

The first label Epstein approached was Decca, one of the most powerful record companies in the U.K., who arranged an audition with the group for January 1, 1962. In the space of three hours, The Beatles recorded 15 tracks. The band was not really satisfied with the performance, but Epstein was convinced it would be enough to secure a deal. However, Decca felt otherwise, rejecting The Beatles because they sounded "too much like The Shadows." Dick Rowe, the head of artists and repertory at Decca, told Brian Epstein that guitar bands were on the way out, a rebuff that John and Paul referred to in a later interview:

Paul: He must be kicking himself now.
John: I hope he kicks himself to death.

While Epstein was furious at Decca's rejection of The Beatles, the band itself was more sanguine: "Don't worry Brian, we'll have to sign to Embassy," John wisecracked. (Embassy was an albums-only label owned by the Woolworth's chain that released out-of-date, low-quality LPs that sold for the price of a single.)

The band's fortune soon changed, however. Epstein hit on the idea of using the Decca audition tapes to make a demonstration disc to play to prospective labels. He paid a visit to the famous HMV store on London's Oxford Street, where it was possible to have one-off records cut from a master tape. The engineer who processed the record took a liking to The Beatles' sound and suggested that Epstein take it to EMI's publishing wing. That same day, Epstein visited EMI's head of publishing, Sid Coleman, who listened to the record and also liked what he heard. He agreed to publish two of the songs—the Lennon/McCartney compositions "Love Of The Loved" and "Hello Little Girl." Furthermore, Coleman agreed to set up a meeting with George Martin, an EMI talent scout and producer.

George Martin was unusual in the pop field in that he'd had classical music training, and had studied at London's Guildhall School of Music. He'd also worked with Spike Milligan and Peter Sellers, two of The Goons—stars of a legendary British radio show of the 1950s. But as rock and roll was the record industry's biggest money-spinner, Martin had reluctantly begun looking for talent among the countless newly formed beat groups. It was with few expectations that he sat down to listen to the latest demo tape to come his way. On the evidence he heard, The Beatles seemed to have little to distinguish them from many other well-rehearsed groups. But he was sufficiently interested to offer them an audition. As he later recalled, "I thought to myself: 'There might just be something there.'"

An impressed George Martin hears a run-through of an early Beatles song at Abbey Road Studios.

The Fab Fourth

The Beatles' Parlophone audition took place on June 6, 1962, at EMI's Abbey Road Studios. Parlophone is one of EMI's subsidiary labels, and up to the early 1960s was best known for producing comedy records. As well as working with Peter Sellers, George Martin had also produced LPs by Peter Ustinov and the cast of the comedy revue *Beyond The Fringe.*

As before, The Beatles concentrated on their usual mix of standards and original material, including an interesting new song called "Love Me Do." George Martin remained unconvinced: he quite liked what he heard, but didn't find it especially exciting. He felt that the old songs the band chose to cover were dull, and that their own material was not obviously commercial enough. However, he was sure about one thing: although Pete Best was fine for live use, he was not a tight enough drummer to use on recordings. If The Beatles were to make records, Martin would insist on using Andy White, his own session drummer. One month later Parlophone signed The Beatles to a one-year contract.

The problem of what to do with Pete Best immediately became a major issue. When the other members found out Martin's views, Paul and George were keen to get rid of Pete just to get the matter out of the way; John was less happy to toe the line. Nevertheless, on August 16, Pete Best was called to Brian Epstein's office and unceremoniously fired, allegedly because his drumming wasn't up to scratch. From then on Best would always be known as pop's ultimate "nearly" man. Unsurprisingly, the incident caused consternation among the band's primarily female fan-base—the drummer was widely regarded as the best-looking Beatle. John, Paul, and George said little about the whole affair.

Once again, The Beatles were drummerless, though not for long. Top of their most-wanted list was Richard Starkey, widely viewed as one of Liverpool's top beat drummers, and better known to *Mersey Beat* readers as Ringo Starr. John later recalled: "Ringo was a professional drummer who performed with one of the top groups in Liverpool before we even had a drummer." Ringo had made a name for himself playing with Rory Storm and the Hurricanes. Like The Beatles, the Hurricanes had honed their craft in the clubs of Hamburg. But Ringo had tired of the discomforts of life on the road and had returned to Liverpool.

He had briefly rejoined the Hurricanes for a summer season in Skegness, northeast England, when he got a call from John Lennon inviting him to join The Beatles. He was told that he'd have to shave off his beard and change his Teddy Boy quiff for a Beatle mop, but that he could keep his sideburns. He agreed.

Ringo made his debut behind the drums for The Beatles on Saturday August 18, 1962, at the Hulme Hall, Port Sunlight, Birkenhead. The "Fab Four" were now complete.

Ringo, bearded and quiffed, during the Hurricanes' residency at Butlin's holiday camp, Skegness.

The beginning of something big

The recording sessions for the first Beatles single were booked for September 6 and 11, 1962. George Martin had already decided that the best way to launch the band would be to use original Lennon/McCartney compositions. He duly selected two tracks from their audition, "P.S. I Love You" and "Love Me Do." The latter, which was to be the single's A-side, featured a harmonica introduction and solo from John.

Since The Beatles' original audition, nobody had thought to tell George Martin that Pete Best had been replaced, so when the group arrived at Abbey Road recording studios they were introduced to Andy White, their drummer for the session. Much to Ringo's distress, his first session with The Beatles was restricted to watching the proceedings from the control room. When Martin eventually heard Ringo drum, he was sufficiently impressed to let him play on the second session, although it still irks Ringo to this day that he wound up playing maracas on the record while Andy White took over on drums. At one point, The Beatles' new drummer started to worry that the rest of the group were willing to sacrifice him as they had Pete Best less than a month before.

On October 5, 1962, "Love Me Do" hit the streets. However, reaching the whole of Britain remained a problem—outside of northwest England, The Beatles were still largely unknown. Brian Epstein came up with a solution. Knowing the number of sales required to get a record into the charts, he bought 10,000 copies of the single through his NEMS record store, enough to earn an appearance in the national *New Musical Express* chart at number 27. By the middle of December "Love Me Do" had reached number 17. A subdued beginning, but at least it brought the group to the attention of a national audience for the first time. In late 1962 the charts were packed with solo singers, mostly American, including Carole King, Bobby Vee, and Little Eva. For a time it must have seemed as though, just as Dick Rowe had predicted, groups with guitars were becoming a thing of the past.

On a more positive note, The Beatles' roadshow was now beginning to build up momentum. Their first Top 20 hit gave them greater confidence in their own material, which henceforth underwent an extraordinary and rapid improvement. From that point on, the songwriting team of John Lennon and Paul McCartney would become ever stronger, eventually developing into the most successful pop partnership of all time. The success of "Love Me Do" also forced George Martin to reassess his opinion of the Liverpudlian foursome. He was now convinced that there was something unique about the group after all, and offered them a five-year contract with Parlophone. Together, George Martin and The Beatles would change the face of popular music forever.

On the brink of success. The Beatles in London, 1962, at the time "Love Me Do" was released.

2 Beatlemania

John Lennon's life is turned upside down in 1963. With hits such as "I Want To Hold Your Hand" and "She Loves You," The Beatles establish themselves as an important new force in pop music. What's more, they stand apart from their contemporaries in that they write most of their own songs. As The Beatles' success spirals out of control, their public appearances are greeted by hordes of screaming teenage girls. The press immediately come up with a new name for this phenomenon: Beatlemania.

The top spot

With "Love Me Do" still in the lower reaches of the Top 30, it was time to record the vital follow-up single. Both Brian Epstein and George Martin were keen on a song brought to them by publisher Dick James. They were convinced that "How Do You Do It?" would be the song to take The Beatles to the top of the charts. But The Beatles themselves had other ideas. John Lennon and Paul McCartney wanted to persevere with their own material, especially their newest number, the bright "Please Please Me," a song that showed off the band's tight vocal harmonies. The track was originally intended as a slow number in the style of Roy Orbison, before Martin suggested the band speed it up. When he heard the results he knew immediately that it was going to be a massive hit. The recording took place on November 26, 1962, and at the end of the session Martin said to the group "Gentlemen, you have just made your first number 1."

When the single appeared in the middle of January 1963, The Beatles made their national TV debut on the Saturday night pop show *Thank Your Lucky Stars*. Further exposure followed on *Juke Box Jury*, a pop show that reviewed new releases.

In the 1960s, the U.K. had several record charts, each of which was based on the sales from selected record stores across the country. Different charts occasionally showed the same single at different positions, depending on the sales registered at a particular store. Most chart guides state that "Please Please Me" reached number 2; however, several of the U.K.'s published record charts, including those in music weeklies *Melody Maker*, *Disc*, and *New Musical Express*, showed the record at number 1, confirming George Martin's prediction. Whatever the position, one thing was clear: with "Please Please Me," The Beatles became a musical force to be reckoned with.

Capitalizing on the momentum of a massive hit single, The Beatles embarked on their first major British tour, though they still found the time for more recording. On February 10, the band traveled down to Abbey Road to record their debut album. George Martin's aim was to capture the energy of their live set. By today's standards the band's work rate was incredible: they began at 10 a.m. and carried on until 11 p.m. In the space of barely 13 hours they recorded an astonishing 79 takes of 14 songs. Eight tracks were Lennon/ McCartney originals; the remaining six were covers from their live show. The session was said to have cost 400 pounds (approximately $600)—a fairly small sum for such a session, even in 1963.

On March 23, 1963, The Beatles' debut album—entitled *Please Please Me* after their hit single—was released. It went straight to the number 1 spot and had sold over half a million copies by the end of the year. The madness had started.

Pop's premier songwriting partnership in the first flush of fame, 1963.

John and Cynthia

Please Please Me was now a national hit. Although The Beatles had broad appeal, Brian Epstein knew that the screaming teenage girls were vital for the group's sustained success and he worked hard to create the illusion that The Beatles were "attainable" to their young female fans. For this fantasy to work, there could be no girlfriends on public display. This was to be a problem for John Lennon. In spite of his wise-guy image and reputation as a rebel, back home in Liverpool John had a wife.

Cynthia Powell had enrolled at Liverpool College of Art at the same time as John. Coming from Hoylake on the Wirral, John quickly marked her out as a "posh kid," though that didn't stop him fancying her. When he asked Cynthia to dance with him at an art school party, she abruptly told him that she was already engaged. "I didn't ask you to marry me, did I?" he shot back. Almost despite herself, Cynthia became increasingly intrigued by this Teddy Boy with a razor-sharp tongue. Her engagement was soon over and before long she and John were dating. The relationship came under stress during The Beatles' spell in Hamburg, when Cynthia would only see John on her occasional visits to Germany, but it really became an issue when The Beatles began to take off. At Brian Epstein's insistence, she was forced to stay in the background.

In August 1962, Cynthia discovered that she was pregnant. Although the timing couldn't have been worse—The Beatles' first single was to be released within two months—John insisted that they be married at once. As unorthodox as he might have been in other respects, John felt compelled to "do the right thing." Thus it was that John Lennon and Cynthia Powell were wed at Mount Pleasant Registry Office on August 23, 1962. Brian Epstein obtained a special marriage license, confident that he could still stop the news from leaking out. Paul was best man; George, Brian, Cynthia's brother Tony, and his wife Marjorie were the only other guests. John's Aunt Mimi, who was furious both at the unplanned pregnancy and the abrupt marriage, which recalled Julia's wedding to Freddy Lennon some 24 years previously, refused to attend. A pneumatic drill outside made much of the wedding ceremony inaudible, causing the participants to become increasingly hysterical with laughter.

On April 8, 1963, Cynthia gave birth to a baby boy—Julian. When The Beatles began the process of moving down to London, it was planned that Cynthia and Julian should return to her mother's home in Hoylake. Before the end of the year, however, Cynthia was tracked down by a reporter and the story of John's marriage and the Lennons' young son broke in the newspapers. Epstein was furious, but John was somewhat relieved that his family no longer had to stay a hidden part of his life.

John and Cynthia, captured as John was becoming one of the most famous pop stars in the world.

Yeah, yeah, yeah!

Nineteen sixty-three was the year that Britain capitulated to the charms of John, Paul, George, and Ringo. Their third single—"From Me To You"—was released on April 11. It went straight to the number 1 spot, selling over half a million copies.

Two weeks later, The Beatles played their biggest gig to date in front of a crowd of 10,000 people at the *New Musical Express* Poll Winners Show, at the Empire Pool, Wembley. The Beatles hadn't actually topped any polls, as the votes were made in 1962, before they'd become a national phenomenon. However, the success of "Please Please Me," "From Me To You," and their debut album meant that their inclusion was a must. And although they were second on the bill to Cliff Richard and the Shadows, the screaming frenzy indicated that much of the audience was there for the Fab Four.

The same thing happened on the national tour that followed. This time The Beatles were supporting Roy Orbison—a true rock-and-roll original and one of their all-time heroes. Within days, however, audience reaction made it clear who the real stars of the show were and the billing order was changed. The Beatles were now a major headlining act.

The British media couldn't get enough of the group. At press conferences each of their distinctive personalities shone through, but more often than not it was the dry scouse wit of John Lennon that captured the headlines. There was also considerable interest in the burgeoning songwriting partnership of Lennon and McCartney. It was unusual enough for a group to write their own songs, rather than having them provided by professional songwriters, but now John and Paul were also scoring hits for other artists. That really was breaking new ground, especially in the U.K.

In August, The Beatles notched up their biggest-ever hit. Indeed, for nearly 20 years "She Loves You" remained the biggest-selling British hit record of all time. (EMI had pressed over 250,000 copies of the single in the month before its release, to cope with demand.) Like many of their classic songs, "She Loves You" was written in a hotel room while the group were on tour. As John and Paul talked and fiddled with their acoustic guitars, John made a crucial suggestion. Instead of writing about "me and you," he reasoned, they should try to come up with something about a third person. As Paul recalled: "We hit on the idea of doing a reported conversation—'She told me what to say, she said she loves you'—giving it a dimension that was different to what we'd done before."

"She Loves You" had all the features that made The Beatles so popular in the first place, plus the instantly memorable "yeah, yeah, yeah" chorus—one of the most famous hook lines in pop history. By the end of the year it had become The Beatles' first million-seller.

The taste of pop, 1963-style. The Beatles' collarless jackets were one of their earliest trademarks.

The Mersey invasion

The buzz surrounding Merseybeat was strong in Liverpool, and it wasn't long before the big London-based record labels heard the sound. Without doubt it was the work of Brian Epstein that gave the new music scene its identity and brought it to national attention.

By early 1963, Epstein's record store was only a small part of his business. He now had a management offshoot, NEMS Enterprises, and signed some of Liverpool's premier acts. At its peak in the early 1960s NEMS represented almost all the major bands in British pop music.

The first Merseybeat band to join The Beatles in the national charts was Gerry and the Pacemakers. Like The Beatles, they had been on the Liverpudlian music scene for a while, having started out as a skiffle act. They even managed to get a number 1 single a few weeks before The Beatles. Ironically, it was their version of Mitch Murray's "How Do You Do It?," the song that The Beatles had turned down in favor of their own "Please Please Me." In an astonishing coup, Gerry and the Pacemakers saw their first three singles—"How Do You Do It?," "I Like It," and "You'll Never Walk Alone"—all go to the top of the national charts.

Other Liverpool bands prominent on the scene at the time were The Fourmost, and Billy J. Kramer and the Dakotas, both of whom achieved several hits, some penned by Lennon and McCartney. The Searchers also enjoyed a substantial career, mostly playing unknown American hits—"Sugar And Spice," "Sweets For My Sweet," and "Needles And Pins" were all Top 2 hits. Another major NEMS artist was Cilla Black, who had a string of U.K. hits before becoming a major TV celebrity later in the decade.

However, Brian's stable of artists faced the problem that he was primarily occupied with The Beatles and had little time to devote to his remaining performers. Within two years most of his other Merseyside acts found that their chart hits had dried up.

Above: The pride of Merseyside. Brian Epstein's stable of NEMS acts in 1963 included The Beatles, Gerry and the Pacemakers, and Billy J. Kramer and the Dakotas. Epstein himself is seated far right. Opposite: Ex-Cavern cloakroom girl Priscilla White found fame as Cilla Black, scoring a number of hits as a solo singer and becoming a major show business star in the U.K.

It's Beatlemania!

By now, The Beatles had become big news. On Monday, November 4, 1963, they played at The Royal Command Performance, regarded by many entertainers at the time as the peak of professional achievement. For this annual British showbiz outing, a cast of top variety artists—singers, comedians, magicians, dancers, and others—perform in front of members of the British royal family. In its heyday, the show was broadcast on a Sunday night and regularly attracted some of the highest annual TV audience figures. Indeed, it was so popular that in a spirit of fair play that characterized the early days of British TV, the two major networks took it in turns to broadcast the show.

The event took place at London's Prince of Wales Theatre in the presence of the Queen Mother, Princess Margaret, and Lord Snowdon. The Beatles' appearance caused a sensation, and not just because of their music. In fact, there were no screams at all from the crowd when they played their opening song, "From Me To You." Paul made the audience titter with a crack about Sophie Tucker being their "favorite American group" before the band played "Till There Was You." However, it was John's comment before their closing number that really stuck in the mind. Before playing their final song, "Twist And Shout," he made a request for audience participation: "On this next number I want you all to join in. Would those in the cheap seats clap their hands. The rest of you can rattle your jewelry." In an environment of social deference, John's comment was considered quite shocking, but it was delivered in such a tongue-in-cheek manner that it could not possibly cause offense.

They had charmed the Establishment. The other acts might just as well have gone home—the newspaper coverage of the evening's performance was mostly devoted to the cheeky Liverpudlian rock-and-roll group. "Beatles Rock The Royals" announced a *Daily Express* headline the next day, while the *Daily Mail* trumpeted a "Night Of Triumph For Four Young Men." John Lennon's line was widely regarded as a piece of good-natured irreverence, a welcome breath of fresh air in the otherwise rather stuffy atmosphere of the Command Performance. The Queen Mother in particular was taken by the group: "They are so fresh and vital. I simply adore them," she enthused. Meeting The Beatles after the show, she asked them where they were performing next. When she was told they were playing in Slough, Her Majesty mischievously replied, "Oh, that's near us." (The royal residence at Windsor Castle is only a short distance from Slough.)

Outside the Prince of Wales Theatre, hordes of screaming teenage fans waited for a glimpse of their idols. Reporting on the mayhem, the *Daily Mirror* coined a new word to describe this latest pop phenomenon—"Beatlemania."

John on stage in 1963, still tantalizingly within reach of the fans, but only just.

John and Brian

Nobody could deny the major part that Brian Epstein played in The Beatles' success; in turn, their success had made him a very wealthy young man. Brian enjoyed the fame and recognition as much as the healthy bank balance; he liked being a public figure. But the public enjoyment of his wealth was in complete contrast to the secrecy with which he conducted his private life. Although his family and friends knew that Brian was homosexual, in such unenlightened times the consequences of that news becoming public knowledge could have had a disastrous effect on his career and on those whom he managed.

There has been much speculation about Brian's relationship with and feelings toward John Lennon. One famous account of The Beatles' story suggests that he fell in love with the leather-clad John when he first saw The Beatles performing at The Cavern and that this had been his motivation for signing the band. While plausible, this theory has been widely refuted by those close to Lennon.

Nevertheless, mystery still surrounds a short holiday that the two men spent together at the end of April 1963. With a break in The Beatles' heavy schedule, but barely three weeks after the birth of his son Julian, John and Brian flew off together to Torremolinos, Spain. Nobody knows for certain what took place during their break, but there has been speculation over the years that the two had a brief affair. Again, nobody who was close to The Beatles' camp believes this to have been true, although that hasn't stopped books and films being based on the idea. At the time, rumors about the holiday subsequently led to one of the ugliest incidents in The Beatles' early career. In June 1963, at Paul McCartney's 21st birthday party in Liverpool, Cavern DJ Bob Wooler teased John about the Spanish holiday, suggesting that he was homosexual. Drunk and in a confrontational mood, John turned on Wooler and beat him up so badly that he had to be hospitalized. Brian drove the battered DJ to the hospital himself, and later made John apologize to Wooler.

In truth, although Brian was only six years older than the oldest Beatle, the band tended to view him rather as a nervous teacher trying to keep a class of unruly kids in order. When his business was a simple matter of getting The Beatles to gigs or recording sessions, there were no problems, but as their popularity spread, Brian found himself increasingly stretched. Although excellent as the band's manager, Brian's inexperience of big business soon became evident. He found that he had less and less time to deal with the details of the band's affairs. Moreover, under pressure, his business decisions were sometimes unwise: for instance, he signed away The Beatles' exclusive merchandising rights for a mere 10 percent, losing himself and the band a hefty fortune in as much time as it takes to give a signature.

Epstein and Lennon; manager and head Beatle talk business during rehearsals for a TV appearance.

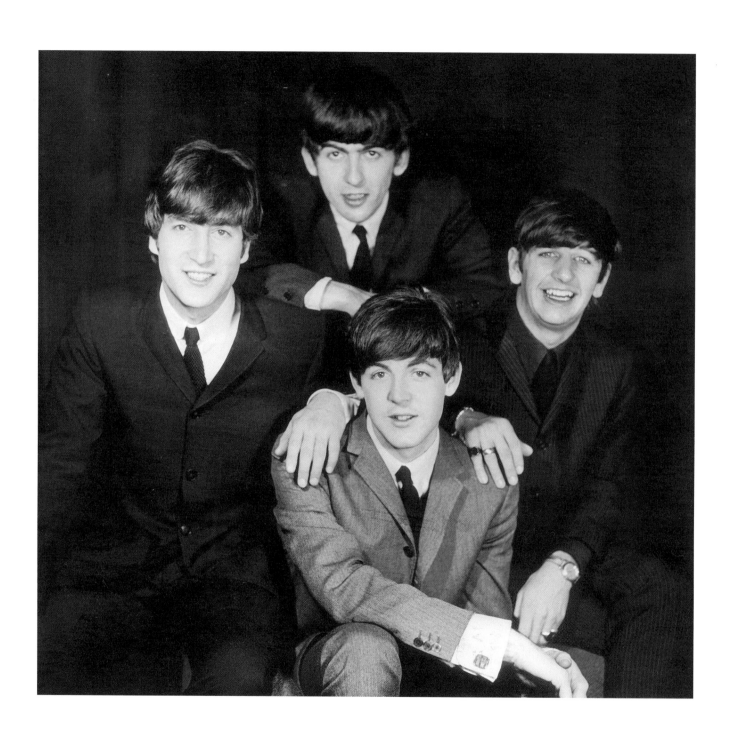

With The Beatles

In August 1963, with "She Loves You" at the top of the singles chart and *Please Please Me* outselling every other album in Britain, The Beatles took time out to record some new material for their second album. Once again, Abbey Road's Studio Two was the home for the sessions. This time the band was given the luxury of three days to finish the entire album. The group was now noticeably more at ease in the studio and John in particular was keen to learn about recording techniques, especially those, such as double-tracking, that could strengthen and improve the sound of his own voice.

Three months later, on November 30, The Beatles' debut album was finally dislodged from the top of the U.K. album charts. The new best-seller was their follow-up, *With The Beatles*, which had received advanced orders of more than a quarter of a million copies. The Beatles' first two albums set a precedent that no other artist has come close to matching: 50 consecutive weeks at the U.K. number 1 spot. *Please Please Me* held out at the top for an incredible 29 weeks, while *With The Beatles* notched up 21 weeks.

With The Beatles was a pioneering album, and the critics again noted the quality of Lennon and McCartney's songs. (Although many of their songs were solo compositions, they were contractually obliged to publish them jointly.) One song, John's "Not A Second Time," was singled out by William Mann, music critic of *The Times*. Mann compared the track to Mahler's "Song of the Earth," observing "One gets the impression that they think simultaneously of harmony and melody, so firmly are the major tonic sevenths and ninths built into their tunes, and the flat submediant key switches, so natural in the Aeolian cadences at the end ...." "I thought Aeolian cadences sounded like exotic birds," John quipped.

The album's cover also set it apart from other pop releases. Brian Epstein commissioned one of Britain's top fashion photographers, Robert Freeman, to provide a jacket image. Freeman produced four moody black-and-white portraits of The Beatles, each one half in shadow. The photographs were arranged on the four quarters of the jacket. In hindsight, the photographs were eerily reminiscent of some of the pictures taken of the five-piece Beatles by Astrid Kirchherr during the group's time in Hamburg.

The Beatles ended an unreal year with another big hit single. "I Want To Hold Your Hand" hit the U.K. top spot with advance orders of over one million copies. In just 12 months the group had stormed the British pop scene and media in a way never seen before or since. They had best-selling records, their haircuts had started a new fashion trend, and the press loved them. But the biggest challenge in Brian Epstein's game plan was still to be faced. As yet, The Beatles meant nothing in the U.S.

By the end of 1963 the Fab Four had become the biggest thing to ever hit the U.K. pop scene.

The Beatles are coming!

Why any American teenager would care about an English pop group was anyone's guess. Pop history offered little in the way of proof that they even knew there was a U.K. music scene at all. Skiffle had remained entirely a British phenomenon, while Cliff Richard and the Shadows, at one point the most popular group in the U.K., meant nothing across the Atlantic. After all, the U.S. had the king of rock and roll, Elvis Presley. They didn't need pallid English imitators such as Cliff, let alone his less successful peers Billy Fury or Marty Wilde. By the end of 1963, The Beatles had conquered their home country, but were far from confident about the chances of their success Stateside. "They've got everything over there," an apprehensive Ringo Starr told the *Liverpool Post*, "will they want us too?" First indications seemed to be that the U.S. didn't much want The Beatles at all.

The Beatles' British label, Parlophone, was part of the mighty EMI corporation that also owned Capitol, one of the biggest labels in the United States. It might have been assumed, therefore, that the mechanism for releasing The Beatles' records in the U.S. was already in place. However, in the days that preceded the "global village" of the modern entertainment industry, there was little in the way of international coordination between Capitol and EMI in the U.K. Capitol Records had heard The Beatles and didn't think much of them. In the end, Brian Epstein took the decision to place the group's first three U.K. hits on small independent labels in the U.S. The singles all sank without trace.

Things took a significant turn when Brian made his first visit to New York and played John and Paul's demo recording of "I Want To Hold Your Hand" to Capitol Records' executives at the company's offices. They remained unconvinced but, given the group's extraordinary success in the U.K., Capitol agreed to give The Beatles a chance.

Help for Brian's efforts to introduce The Beatles to America came from an unexpected source. Ed Sullivan had a nationwide television show that for the previous 10 years had launched many celebrities, including Elvis Presley, into the national consciousness. Whereas Capitol seemed unaware of the pandemonium that surrounded The Beatles in the U.K., Sullivan had experienced it firsthand when a flight he was on from London had been delayed by fans awaiting The Beatles' return from a European tour. Sullivan was impressed that a pop group could have such an impact and could see no reason why the same thing shouldn't be repeated across the Atlantic. He offered to book the group on two of his shows in February 1964. The Beatles' fee for the performance was $3,000. Although Brian was unaware of it at the time, this was a small figure, even for an unknown band. However, it turned out to be one of the most important steps in the band's career.

All set for the States: The Beatles and Brian Epstein at Heathrow Airport on February 7, 1964.

Beatles in the U.S.

The Beatles began 1964 with a low-key tour of France. On January 16, while they were in Paris, Brian Epstein received a telegram from Capitol Records in New York. After making steady progress in the lower reaches of the U.S. charts, "I Want To Hold Your Hand" had suddenly leaped from number 43 to the top position. Although now accustomed to breaking the pop rule book, The Beatles were stunned by the news. With their appearance on the *Ed Sullivan Show* booked for February, they hardly knew what to expect.

Across the Atlantic, a massive publicity campaign was being launched. Posters and windshield stickers everywhere proclaimed "The Beatles Are Coming." English businessman Nicky Byrne, who had bought the exclusive merchandising rights to The Beatles, set up an office in New York, determined to make the best of his new deal. Byrne wanted the band to arrive in a blaze of publicity and had planned his own campaign accordingly. He had thousands of T-shirts printed and took out adverts on prominent New York radio stations. The final touch was a tempting offer to New York's youth: any teenager who went to John F. Kennedy airport to greet The Beatles would receive a free T-shirt and a dollar bill.

The scenes that greeted Pan Am flight 101 as it arrived in New York on February 7 were unprecedented. As The Beatles began to climb down the steps from the plane, they were greeted by 5,000 screaming fans. A 100-man police cordon was called in to hold back the surging mass. At first the Fab Four could not believe that the reception was for them—they presumed the President must be landing. The group was immediately led to a press conference, to face a crowd of 200 New York journalists. Despite the chaos surrounding them, The Beatles fielded every question with their trademark sharp-witted humor. Exchanges were bright and friendly, with each of John's one-liners being met with laughter or even applause. The Beatles had made a good impression at their first meeting with the American public. When the questions were over, the Fabs were lifted into a chauffeur-driven Cadillac by two policemen and whisked off to their hotel, the Plaza, facing Central Park.

On Sunday, February 9, 1964, two days after their arrival, The Beatles gave their first performance on American soil, and in so doing effectively conquered the U.S. The chosen venue was Studio 50—The Ed Sullivan Theater. The show began at 8 p.m. with a dramatic announcement from Mr. Sullivan himself:

"Yesterday and today our theater has been jammed with newspapers and hundreds of photographers from all over the nation. These veterans agree with me that this city never has witnessed the excitement created by these four youngsters from Liverpool who call themselves The Beatles ... Ladies and Gentlemen, THE BEATLES."

Ed Sullivan tries out Paul's bass guitar at rehearsals for The Beatles' U.S. TV debut.

Storming the States

Before the end of Sullivan's introduction a massive scream erupted from the studio audience. Paul counted the band in and they launched into "All My Loving," quickly followed by their cover of "Till There Was You," and then "She Loves You." During their second song, the camera gave each of The Beatles an individual close-up, displaying his name on the screen. John's introduction came with an additional line of information: "Sorry girls, he's married." Later on in the hour-long program, they played "I Saw Her Standing There" and their U.S. chart-topper "I Want To Hold Your Hand."

The Beatles were thrilled by the crowd's reaction, but the pièce de résistance came after their first set. Sullivan held up a telegram from Elvis Presley sent by his manager Colonel Tom Parker, wishing them success on their first visit to America.

The program made television history. The Nielsen Ratings system calculated that the *Ed Sullivan Show* had been watched by 73 million people in 24 million households. This meant that more than 60 percent of all TV viewers in the U.S.—the world's largest TV audience—had tuned in to watch them play. At the end of their first U.S. jaunt, George Harrison commented: "Afterwards they told us that there was no reported crime. Even the criminals had a rest for 10 minutes while we were on."

Not everyone was convinced by the group, however. Ed Sullivan's musical director, Ed Block, saw nothing new in the Fab Four: "The only thing that's different is the hair, as far as I can see," he grouched to the *New York Times*. "I give them a year." Sullivan himself reprimanded Block for his comments.

While they were in the U.S., The Beatles also played a series of high-profile concerts at Washington's Coliseum and New York's famous Carnegie Hall. All met with the same rapturous response. After their Carnegie Hall appearance, U.S. promoter Sid Bernstein tried to secure The Beatles for an appearance at Madison Square Garden a few days later. Bernstein offered Brian Epstein $25,000 and a $5,000 donation to the British Cancer Fund, but Epstein declined, telling the promoter "Let's leave this for next time."

During February 1964 America became besotted with The Beatles. The early singles that had bombed on release were now being repromoted. By the beginning of April, the *Billboard* charts had been besieged by Britain's top group. Not content with holding numbers 1 and 2 in the album charts, The Beatles also had the top five best-selling singles in the U.S., as well as entries at 31, 41, 46, 58, 65, 68, and 79. That's 12 singles in the *Billboard* Hot 100. No artist in the history of popular music had come anywhere near this level of domination. And it's difficult to imagine that it could ever happen again.

The Beatles leave New York's Carnegie Hall after a triumphant performance on February 12, 1964.

And now the world

Having conquered the U.S., in June 1964 The Beatles took on the rest of the world, which succumbed to them as completely as the States had. Dates in Scandinavia were followed by a flight to East Asia and Australia. The chaotic scenes that greeted them were by now becoming familiar. On their flight from Hong Kong to Sydney, The Beatles made an unscheduled refueling stop at Darwin in the north of Australia. Here, even at 2 a.m., a crowd of 400 screaming fans appeared as if from nowhere to greet them.

In the middle of August, after spending a few days at Abbey Road recording tracks for another new album, The Beatles set off on their first major tour of the U.S. The reception awaiting them there was even more hysterical than before. When their plane touched down in San Francisco, they were met by 9,000 ecstatic fans and had to be transported from the airport in a massive iron crate for their own safety. On a more positive note, by now they were reaping the rewards of their unprecedented success and were able to move from city to city in a hired jet plane.

The band were already beginning to view their concerts as something of a joke—they were rarely able to hear themselves play above the constant screams of their fans, and their music suffered as a result. The situation began to affect John in particular. In the odd off-guard moment, the Beatle pleasantries would slip, and the cynical side of John Lennon emerged: "It wouldn't matter if I never sang. Often I don't anyway," he revealed in one interview. "I just stand there and make mouth movements .... I reckon we could send out four waxwork dummies of ourselves and that would satisfy the crowds. Beatles concerts are nothing to do with music anymore. They're just bloody tribal rites."

For the moment, all four Fabs were willing to play the game, but their lifestyle was becoming increasingly abnormal. Feted wherever they went, the group was showered with the kind of adulation more usually reserved for royalty, or gods. As George Martin recalled, "in some places they'd wheel in paraplegics who were brought in to touch them—it was like Jesus, almost." Their private lives were nonexistent and the four young men began to feel more and more like prisoners of their own success: "The only place we ever had any peace was when we got back to the hotel suite, and went to the bathroom!" George Harrison recalled, somewhat ruefully, when the tour was over.

The Beatles stayed in the U.S. for just over a month. They played 25 dates in 34 days in 24 cities, created havoc, and then went home. With only enough time to slot in overdubs for the new album and to record a new A-side, their phenomenal workload continued with another major British tour. Sustaining Beatlemania was proving to be a full-time job.

The eye of the hurricane: The Beatles and Brian Epstein savor a rare moment of peace, 1964.

A Hard Day's Night

By 1964 The Beatles were pop music's biggest act, but Brian Epstein was already preparing the next phase of his master plan. He felt that the time was now right for The Beatles to hit the silver screen, and quickly agreed a three-film deal with the United Artists company.

The working title for The Beatles' debut film, "Beatlemania," was later dropped in favor of "A Hard Day's Night"—one of Ringo's many idiosyncratic phrases. Director Richard Lester was given the task of transferring the group's knockabout humor to the big screen. John Lennon in particular was pleased with the choice—the director's best-known work so far had been an 11-minute feature entitled *The Running, Jumping And Standing Still Film* (1959), featuring Spike Milligan and Peter Sellers, two of John's radio heroes, from *The Goon Show*. The film script was written by Alun Owen, a playwright with a reputation based on a series of gritty TV dramas set in Liverpool.

The storyline was a simple one. The Beatles were to play themselves in a series of scenarios that mimicked incidents in their own hectic lives. *A Hard Day's Night* included many aspects of The Beatles' inimitable style, such as their familiar press conference wisecracks and Marx Brothers-like clowning. The film skillfully created the impression that audiences were seeing The Beatles making the whole thing up as they went along. In reality, the film was tightly scripted and John fought hard to get his own contributions included: "We were a bit infuriated by the glibness of the dialog and we were always trying to get it more realistic, but they [Lester and Owen] wouldn't have it," he complained later.

Both before and since The Beatles, most films built around pop stars have been something of a letdown—witness Elvis Presley's string of movies, which after a promising start degenerated into formulaic flops. By contrast, *A Hard Day's Night* proved to be both a critical winner and an international hit, earning $14 million on its first release. A number of foreign-language versions of the film went out under alternative titles. In Germany, where The Beatles had enjoyed two hits in translation—"Komm, Gib Mir Deine Hand" and "Sie Liebt Dich"—the film was issued as *Yeah Yeah Yeah, Die Beatles*. Italians saw the film as *Tutti Per Uno*, and the French as *Quatre Garçons Dans Le Vent*.

Accompanying the film was the inevitable soundtrack album, which this time featured The Beatles' first set of entirely self-penned numbers. It was clear that John in particular was finding a more serious voice as a songwriter. Widely perceived as the band's leader, he was largely responsible for seven of the eight new numbers. The album *A Hard Day's Night* and the single of the same name sold in vast quantities the world over, while the film's success suggested that The Beatles might become significant as more than just a pop group.

Man in the mirror: John meets John in a reflective moment from *A Hard Day's Night*, 1964.

Meeting Bob Dylan

The Beatles became a global phenomenon in 1964. However, the exhausting lifestyle that they now led was beginning to tell on their music. The year ended with a new album—*Beatles For Sale*—which many critics regarded as something of a disappointment. John and Paul didn't have enough high-quality original material for the LP and so reverted to filling the holes with cover versions.

John's contributions to *Beatles For Sale* revealed a darker side to his writing. This can be heard clearly in the album's three opening tracks: "No Reply," "I'm A Loser," and "Baby's In Black." The pressure of Beatlemania was beginning to tell.

A new influence was detectable in some of the songs on *Beatles For Sale*. The Beatles had their introduction to the music of Bob Dylan when they first hit the U.S., and he made a big impact on them. John remembered their initial meeting, on August 28, 1964, at New York's Delmonico Hotel: "He was always saying 'Listen to the words, man' and I said 'I can't be bothered. I listen to the overall sound.'" But John was the first to admit that Dylan had helped him to think more seriously about his lyrics. John had always thought of himself as something of a wordsmith, but in his eyes Dylan was in a league of his own. This was to be the start of what John himself called his "Dylan period," during which his songs became more introspective. His singing voice even acquired something of Dylan's nasal whine.

The meeting with Dylan was to have further consequences. It was he who introduced The Beatles to marijuana—a drug that hadn't made much of an impact in Britain thus far. Ironically, Dylan had taken The Beatles' breakthrough U.S. single, "I Want To Hold Your Hand," as proof that the Fab Four were already hip to joints. He had misheard the lines "I can't hide, I can't hide" and thought The Beatles were singing "I get high, I get high." After Dylan gave The Beatles their first taste of marijuana, John developed an appetite for any substance that might provide an altered state, boost his creativity, or—when he felt the need—obliterate the pressure of being a Beatle. Shortly afterward, the hallucinogenic drug lysergic acid diethylamide, better known as LSD, was to make a major impression on him; its influence can be heard in much of The Beatles' later music, especially their crowning glory, *Sgt. Pepper's Lonely Hearts Club Band*.

John's wife Cynthia had little interest in sharing her husband's new pursuits. Indeed, to her mind, drugs played a big part in the subsequent breakup of their marriage. "We were on different mental planes," she later reflected. "John's thoughts would always be more expansive than mine ... he kept saying that on his trips he was seeing beautiful things."

Folk troubadour Bob Dylan in 1964. His groundbreaking approach to lyrics made a major impact on John Lennon, whose songwriting fell heavily under the influence of Dylan in the mid-1960s.

Second thoughts

Nineteen sixty-five was to be a year of transition for the group. The Beatlemania frenzy that had characterized the previous two years was beginning to slow down. As far as the group's manager was concerned, though, there was to be no letting up. The coming year was to include another major tour of the U.S. as well as a second feature film. However, for the first time in the band's career, The Beatles themselves were beginning to have second thoughts about the whole business and to wonder how they might break the unrelenting treadmill of new albums followed by grueling tours.

The Beatles had paid their dues as a live band in Hamburg and Liverpool, and when the first wave of Beatlemania broke, they initially enjoyed the experience. After all, they'd earned the adulation. However, by mid-1965 they had lost their enthusiasm for live performances. Whereas once they had been proud of being a tight, accomplished band, nowadays all they could hear when they performed was the incessant screaming of the audience. As The Beatles began to take less of an interest in playing live music, the quality of their onstage performances began to deteriorate. Ringo took to drumming on the offbeat, to keep himself interested. John, who had always jokingly told the screaming fans to "Shaddup!," was more inclined to yell obscenities at the audience when he was away from the concert microphone.

Behind closed doors, The Beatles all agreed that changes were needed. They wanted to reduce the amount of time they toured; significantly, they wanted to devise more time for songwriting and recording. The Beatles had been studio novices when they first met George Martin. Now, over two years later, they were comfortable enough at Abbey Road Studios to want to experiment at greater length with the possibilities of recording. These seeds of discontent would soon transform The Beatles from mere teen idols into, arguably, the greatest artists in the history of popular music.

When he wasn't on the road, John settled into "Kenwood," his newly acquired mock-Tudor mansion in Surrey, with Cynthia and his young son Julian. Although to the public he was the most controversial and provocative Beatle, John was a home bird at heart, happy lounging on a sofa watching TV, reading, or listening to records. In reality, he was feeling more uncomfortable with Beatlemania than the others. He began to lose interest in his public persona and started putting on weight, developing a puffy roundness to his face. At first Cynthia interpreted this as a sign of domestic contentment, but even though he seemed to have the world at his feet, John Lennon was not happy with his life. His feelings were summed up neatly in a new song he'd just written—"Help!"

The Beatles' second U.S. tour, 1965—despite the smile, Beatlemania was starting to wear John down.

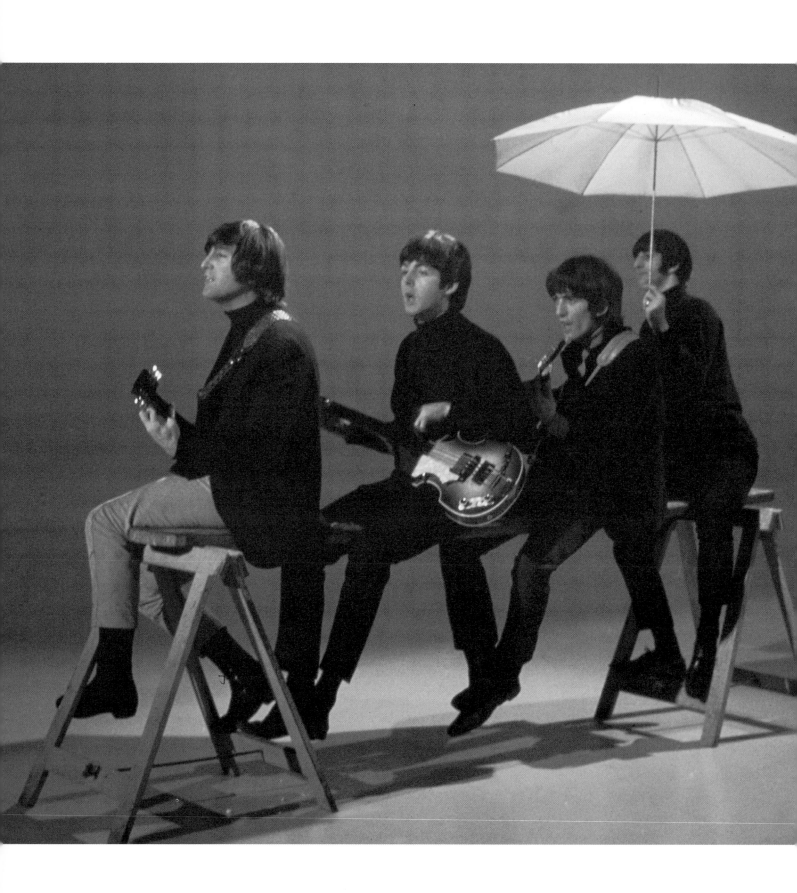

Help!

A *Hard Day's Night* had proved to be more successful—both commercially and artistically—than anyone involved in the film could have hoped for. But The Beatles' next movie, *Help!*, was to be a much less satisfying experience.

Richard Lester was once again at the helm, and a new scriptwriter—the highly rated Marc Behm—was brought in. But unlike *A Hard Day's Night* author Alun Owen, Behm had little understanding of The Beatles' native scouse humor. What he produced may have been funny in its own right, but it failed to capture the essence of the band's laconic in-jokes.

Above: Filming *Help!* in Austria, March 1965.

The plot centers on a religious cult that discovers a sacrificial ring has gone missing—in fact, it has been sent to Ringo by a fan. Ringo is unable to remove the ring from his finger and so The Beatles are pursued for the rest of the film by members of the cult, who seek to recapture the ring, by fair means or foul.

The Beatles acquitted themselves capably enough, their relaxed performances doubtless influenced by their habit of sneaking off for a quick joint between takes. But as far as John was concerned, "*Help!* was a drag, because we didn't know what was happening ... we were on pot by then and all the best stuff is on the cutting-room floor, with us breaking up all over the place." On another occasion he declared that the film was "just bullshit."

Help! was The Beatles' last feature film—at least, the last in which they acted. Contractually tied to a third film, Brian Epstein commissioned a script from British playwright Joe Orton, at the time the toast of London for scandalous comedies such as *Loot* and *Entertaining Mr. Sloane*. The project failed to get off the ground, as much due to The Beatles' refusal to drag themselves through the filmmaking process one more time as to any problems with the script itself, although the latter was sexually and politically controversial. After Orton's violent death in 1967, the script was published as *Up Against It*.

The U.K. album that accompanied *Help!* was structured so that only the first side featured songs used in the film. The LP featured two multimillion-selling singles, the title track and John's memorable "Ticket To Ride," a song he subsequently described as "one of the earliest heavy metal records ever made." Among the lesser fare on the flip side sat Paul McCartney's "Yesterday." Although the latter was not released as a single in Britain at the time, it has since become one of The Beatles' most famous songs, ending up as the most recorded song of the twentieth century.

Opposite: The Beatles in a promotional film for their single "Help!," 1965.

Man of words

John had always been interested in creative writing. Even in the bottom-stream English class at Quarry Bank, he amused himself with his own nonsense verse and short stories that were kept in an exercise book he called the "Daily Howl." In Liverpool, as the pop scene and The Beatles were taking off, his poems, spoof personal ads, and musings were often published in the city's own music paper, *Mersey Beat.*

By 1965, John had forged a reputation as the Beatle who gave his group an edge. At press conferences all four were lively and sharp-witted, but John was always prepared to go one step further, his statements shot through with a bluntness rare in pop stars of the mid-1960s:

"I don't suppose I think much about the future. I don't really give a damn. It's selfish but I don't care too much for humanity."

"I get spasms of being intellectual. I read a bit about politics but I don't think I'd vote for anyone. No message from any of those phony politicians is coming through to me."

Above: A page from John's notebook, the "Daily Howl."

At the height of The Beatles' fame, John produced two books of his own poetry, prose, and doodles; both became best-sellers, enhancing his status as the "intellectual" Beatle. The inventive wordplay of *In His Own Write*, published in March 1964, was inspired by The Goons, Lewis Carroll, and the English linguistic comedian "Professor" Stanley Unwin, who made a career out of spouting indecipherable gobbledygook. *The Times Literary Supplement* called it "Worth the attention of anyone who fears the impoverishment of the English language and the British imagination." The follow-up, *A Spaniard In The Works*, was published the following year and was a more considered collection. Whereas John's debut had been a compilation of pieces created for his own amusement, the second was written to order. Once again, however, his sense of the ridiculous was well to the fore, with stories such as "Snore Wife and Some Several Dwarts" and his "Last Will and Testicle."

John's approach to writing echoed that of his attitude to making music. He summed it up in an interview for BBC radio's *World Of Books* program: "publishers sometimes say 'Should we leave this out or change that?' And I fight like mad because once I've done it, I like to keep it ... I seldom take something out, so it's spontaneous."

Opposite: The Beatles are apparently divided over the literary merits of *In His Own Write*.

Fame and fortune

Wealth and fame brought about enormous changes for The Beatles. They were all now millionaires. John and Ringo both had mansions in southeast England, where most of their neighbors were lawyers, stockbrokers, and businessmen. George bought a bungalow in a similar area. Only Paul broke the pattern, keeping a London base by buying a property in St. John's Wood, a few minutes' walk from the Abbey Road studios.

On the whole, John adapted easily to the upmarket lifestyle. His home on St. George's Hill in Weybridge was a genuine pop star's mansion, complete with swimming pool. Parked outside was a Rolls-Royce fitted with tinted black windows. The interior decoration at Kenwood reflected both John's wealth and his unorthodoxy, with rooms lined in purple velvet, as well as one painted in bizarre stripes of pink and green. On one wall hung two pictures by his old friend Stuart Sutcliffe.

John enjoyed using his wealth to indulge himself, and others too, gaining a reputation as an extremely generous tipper in restaurants and clubs. However, he occasionally worried that he was never able to tell how much money he was really worth, and that he might be overspending. At one point, concerned that he'd been too extravagant on his car collection, he put his Mini and Ferrari up for sale—"Then one of the accountants said I was all right, so I got the cars back from the showroom."

However, the extent of The Beatles' success still occasionally caught even them by surprise. After their conquest of the U.S., Liverpool's four most famous sons were given a civic reception at the city's Town Hall. When The Beatles arrived, John was stunned to find that 100,000 screaming fans had turned out to greet them. Returning secretly to see his Aunt Mimi, he was horrified to discover that Mendips—his childhood home—was now a shrine, sought out by fans and journalists from across the globe. His aunt no longer had any privacy whatsoever: "I kept changing the phone number, but the fans would keep discovering the new one within a few days," she remembered years later.

Eventually, John invited Mimi to stay with him at Kenwood and told her that he wanted to buy her a new home. He asked her where she wanted to live; the first place that came into her head was Bournemouth, on the south coast of England. That same morning, John and Mimi set off in his chauffeur-driven Rolls-Royce to visit properties in the area and within hours he had bought her a bungalow overlooking Poole Harbour. He gave her a plaque to put on the wall, inscribed with her old warning to him: "The guitar's all very well, John, but you'll never make a living out of it."

As well as a Rolls-Royce, John already owned a Ferrari and a black Mini Cooper before he passed his driving test on February 15, 1965. Cars were always to be a major passion in his life.

The new "establishment"

Each year, the Queen of England's official birthday is accompanied by an announcement of those Britons who are to receive knighthoods and other honors. Typically, the list of recipients includes military men, politicians, civil servants, and businessmen. However, in 1965, four unlikely awardees were singled out for attention. Each of The Beatles was to receive the MBE—The Membership of the Most Excellent Order of the British Empire.

The popular press approved the decision—"She Loves Them, Yeah! Yeah! Yeah!" ran a *Daily Mirror* headline. Other members of British society, however, were less enthusiastic about the announcement. One military hero, Colonel Frederick Wagg, was furious at the award. In his anger he returned 12 of his medals, resigned from the Labour Party (Labour prime minister Harold Wilson was responsible for suggesting to Her Majesty that The Beatles receive the awards), and canceled a large contribution to party funds. Ex-RAF squadron leader Paul Pearson returned his MBE "because it had become debased."

The Beatles themselves were rather baffled by the award. "I thought you had to drive tanks and win wars to get an MBE," a bemused John Lennon confessed. But he was clearly irritated by the protesters. As far as he was concerned, army officers were given the award for killing people: "We got ours for entertaining. On balance I'd say we deserve ours more."

Lennon remained ambivalent about the award: "Taking the MBE was a sellout for me," he later admitted. "Before you get an MBE the Palace writes to you to ask if you're going to accept it, because you're not supposed to reject it publicly .... Brian and a few other people persuaded me that it was in our interests to take it ... but I'm glad, really, that I did accept it because it meant that four years later I could use it to make a gesture." (In 1969 he would return the medal as, among other things, a protest at British foreign policy.)

The Beatles' investiture took place at Buckingham Palace on October 26, 1965. Outside Buckingham Palace 4,000 screaming fans were held back by the police. After the ceremony The Beatles displayed their silver crosses to the press. Paul said that the Queen was "very friendly. She was like a mum to us," and that the Palace was a "keen pad."

In 1970, during an interview with French magazine *L'Express*, John claimed that The Beatles had all smoked marijuana in the toilets of Buckingham Palace before the ceremony—an episode that the other three have always strenuously denied.

Opposite: The Beatles receive their MBEs—October 26, 1965.
Right: Storming the gates. The Beatles' investiture provoked frantic scenes outside Buckingham Palace.

Back in the U.S.

A matter of days after the premiere of *Help!* The Beatles returned to the United States for the third time. Although they were only away for two weeks, and their departures and arrivals were now creating slightly less havoc, it was still an arduous ordeal.

The first date, Sunday, August 15, took place at the William A. Shea Municipal Stadium, home of the New York Mets baseball team. Since both the concert and surrounding events were being filmed for a TV documentary, the producers planned to make the band's entrance as dramatic as possible. The original idea was to have the band flown into the stadium by helicopter, but the authorities saw this as potentially dangerous. Instead, the Fab Four rode in a limousine from their hotel to a helipad along the Hudson River. From there they were flown to the site of the World's Fair, in Queens, not far from the stadium. They completed their journey in a Wells Fargo armored truck. At 9:16 p.m.—to the deafening screams of over 55,000 fans—The Beatles entered the arena by running through the players' tunnel, climbed the steps onto the stage, plugged in their guitars, and launched into the opening riff of "Twist And Shout." Seemingly swept along by the spectacle, The Beatles gave one of their most powerfully energetic performances ever that night. The resulting film of the occasion, *The Beatles At Shea Stadium*, is a unique record not only of The Beatles performing some of their greatest hits, but also of the very essence of Beatlemania.

The Shea Stadium concert represented the pinnacle of The Beatles' popularity as performers and the statistics surrounding their appearance were a catalog of superlatives. The crowd of 55,600 fans was at that time the largest ever assembled for a concert. The box-office receipts, $304,000, were the highest yet taken and the band's own share of the takings, $160,000, was the most any artist had earned for a single concert.

Unsurprisingly, the remainder of the tour lacked the zest of that opening triumph. John in particular had begun to hate touring. It didn't matter where in the world The Beatles went, they were now far too famous to travel as ordinary citizens. The routine was always the same: airport; police convoy; hotel room; police convoy; stadium; police convoy; hotel room; police convoy; airport. As John later observed: "The bigger we got, the more unreality we had to face, and the more you were expected to do."

There was also the very real danger that they would be physically harmed. Arriving in Houston at 2 a.m. on August 18, The Beatles' airplane was surrounded by fans as it taxied in. The fans clambered onto the plane to be near their heroes; some were even smoking next to the plane's fuel tanks. And every new city brought more of the same madness.

The Beatles' appearance at Shea Stadium in 1965 saw them play to the largest audience that had ever gathered for a pop concert up to that time.

A new sophistication

After their latest conquest of the States, The Beatles were allowed the luxury of a six-week holiday. Although George and Ringo were able to get away for a bit, the break was not as relaxing for John and Paul. Less inclined than ever to compose new material during their U.S. tour, they now found themselves with another album to write.

The result was the transitional *Rubber Soul.* As George Martin observed: "It was the first album to present a new, growing Beatles to the world." It also clearly showcased the diverging talents of the band's creative axis. Paul McCartney had now become a classic tunesmith in his own right, but it was John who seemed to be making the more interesting moves. Compositions such as "Norwegian Wood (This Bird Has Flown)" were evidence of his continuing fascination with Bob Dylan, featuring strummed acoustic guitars and increasingly personal lyrics. Few people realized quite how personal they were: "I was trying to write about an affair without letting me [sic] wife know," he later confessed, discussing "Norwegian Wood." "I was sort of writing it from my own experiences, girls' flats, things like that." Similarly, on "Nowhere Man," with its rich vocal harmonies and sophisticated arrangement, John's lyrics speak volumes about the boredom, lack of direction, and lack of faith that were increasingly creeping into his life. Songs such as "Girl" and "Run For Your Life" attracted much critical flak for their supposed misogyny, an accusation that John was to spend many years trying to shake off. The album also featured one of his very best songs— the wonderfully understated "In My Life"—in which he reflected fondly on past loves and friends. George Martin added a harpsichordlike keyboard solo in the middle, providing the song with an unexpected but memorable twist.

Rubber Soul was also notable in that it featured no album "filler." All the songs were strong, most were innovative in their use of instrumentation or in their structure, and there were no cover versions or previously released tracks. Brian Wilson of The Beach Boys was so impressed with the high standard maintained throughout the record that he set about creating his own filler-free LP, and came up with *Pet Sounds*, generally regarded as The Beach Boys' masterpiece and one of the finest pop albums of all time.

Years later, John saw *Rubber Soul* as a crucial stage in The Beatles' development, arguing that both technically and musically they felt themselves to be improving, until at last they became the dominant force in the studio: "In the early days we had to take what we were given ... we were learning the techniques on *Rubber Soul*. We were more precise about making that album, and we took over the cover and everything ...." The Beatles were taking pop music and making an art form out of it.

By 1965 The Beatles were no longer merely teen pin-ups; they had become pop pioneers.

3 From Pop to Art

With the release of *Revolver* in 1966, The Beatles reach a new peak of creativity. For the first time, critics begin treating the work of a pop group as serious art. It is the start of an unprecedented string of definitive recordings that include *Sgt. Pepper's Lonely Hearts Club Band*—still viewed by many as the greatest album of all time.

Serious young men

Although they were only in their mid-twenties, the four Beatles had experienced three chaotic years of unrivaled success. And just a passing glance at the cover of *Rubber Soul* was enough to see that changes were in the air. Photographed through a then fashionable "fish-eye" lens, the happy-go-lucky mop tops of old had become four serious-looking young men, unsmiling, and coolly decked out in suede. The pressure to keep on supplying the product was visibly taking its toll.

Nevertheless, 1965 ended in triumph for the group. On the same day that *Rubber Soul* was released, a classic, double A-sided single emerged: John's "Day Tripper" backed with Paul's "We Can Work It Out"—unusually, neither track appeared on the album. The title of the former was a knowing reference to those who were not as initiated into drug culture as The Beatles and their peers—a "Sunday driver" by another name. "We Can Work It Out" was primarily Paul's work, though John supplied the world-weary middle eight of "Life is very short" as a complement to his partner's upbeat, optimistic sentiments in the rest of the song. To satisfy the expected demand in the U.K., EMI pressed 750,000 copies of the record.

As was now traditional, both single and album leaped straight to the number 1 spot on both sides of the Atlantic. Furthermore, *Rubber Soul* scored unanimous critical acclaim from the serious music press. In America, the album broke all sales records, selling 1.2 million copies within the first nine days of its release. Beatlemania may have been on the wane, but the fans were still queuing up outside the record stores and The Beatles seemed to be able to effortlessly combine commercial success with critical acclaim—a rare achievement.

Of course, it was hardly exceptional for a group of teenage idols to want to produce work of greater sophistication as they matured. More often than not, however, such moves resulted in derision from music critics and the alienation of the group's audiences. As in so much else, The Beatles were to prove a significant exception to the rule. The widespread critical praise heaped on *Rubber Soul* gave the group vital encouragement and the confidence to expand their music into uncharted territories. The group's music was growing up and, if sales were anything to go by, the fans were growing with it. The Beatles were now beginning to appeal to a wider, more culturally aware audience.

Significantly, the day "We Can Work It Out"/"Day Tripper" and *Rubber Soul* were released in the U.K., the group began their last British tour. More than ever, the four Beatles were now convinced that it was the recording studio, rather than the stage, on which their future triumphs would depend. *Rubber Soul* proved to be the first in a run of classic albums that no other band has come close to matching.

John Lennon in the mid-1960s, when The Beatles abandoned the stage for the recording studio.

Bigger than Jesus?

The first half of 1966 was relatively quiet by Beatle standards. Much of the time was spent in the studio working on a follow-up to the massively successful *Rubber Soul*. In July 1966, however, John Lennon hit the news headlines as never before. And this time the publicity had nothing to do with his music.

Six months earlier, John had given an interview to the *London Evening Standard*'s Maureen Cleave, a long-standing friend of The Beatles. During their conversation, John talked openly about his views on organized religion, remarking: "Christianity will go. It will vanish and shrink. I needn't argue with that .... We're more popular than Jesus now." The interview was published in January 1966, to little reaction from the British public.

The problems started when an American teenage magazine, *Datebook*, bought Maureen Cleave's interview and published John's comments under the banner "I don't know which will go first—rock and roll or Christianity." His quote caused an uproar that quickly swept through the United States. Stoked by support from the right-wing Christian lobby, thousands of American church-goers were encouraged to take matters into their own hands. Radio station after radio station—and not just those in the traditional Bible Belt—banned The Beatles' music. In addition, many right-wing churches organized public burnings of Beatle records and magazines featuring the group.

Arriving in the States at the start of August for what no one at the time realized would be their final tour, The Beatles held a press conference as usual. This time, however, the assembled journalists had only one question to ask. John explained what he had meant by his comments several times over, but the press simply wanted to know whether the head Beatle was prepared to retract his words. Looking pale and harried, John set about trying to put his words into some kind of context:

"I'm not anti-God, anti-Christ, or antireligion," he stressed. "I was not saying we are greater or better ... I said 'Beatles' because it's easy for me to talk about Beatles. I could have said 'TV' or 'the cinema' or anything popular and I would have got away with it." Clearly the wave of anger aroused by his comments had shocked the usually cocky Lennon. With as much good grace as he could summon, he finally conceded "I'm sorry I said it."

A British interviewer later asked John why he'd chosen to make an apology when he'd clearly said nothing wrong. "If I were at the stage I was five years ago I would have shouted 'We'll never tour again' and packed myself off—Lord knows, I don't need the money," he replied. "But the record burning? That was a real shock. I couldn't go away knowing I'd created another little place of hate in the world ... not when I could do something about it."

Teenagers from Jackson, Mississippi, engage in a "ban The Beatles" bonfire, fall 1966.

Revolver

August 1966 saw another milestone for The Beatles, with the release of *Revolver*. Earlier in the year, they had spent three months working on the album at Abbey Road. These days, of course, it can take some artists that long to make a single, but in 1966 such an approach was practically unheard of. Nevertheless, it was time well spent. *Revolver* represented an incredible leap forward from the songs the band had produced just a few years earlier.

As a part of the London "scene," The Beatles now moved in sophisticated circles, and their outlook had changed. "We've all got interested in things that never used to occur to us," Paul McCartney revealed in an interview earlier that year. So it was that under the influence of the fledgling hippy underground, LSD, electronic music, experimental cinema, and the avant-garde art scene, The Beatles' music took a new direction.

Revolver was full of experimentation. Many of the songs were actually "created" in the studio, the recording process itself shaping the final compositions—witness the tape loops used in John's psychedelic masterpiece "Tomorrow Never Knows." Little thought was given to how a four-piece beat group might perform the songs in concert: McCartney's "Eleanor Rigby," one of the album's many highlights, consists only of voices and a string quartet.

And the songs themselves had changed, both in subject matter and form. As writers, Lennon and McCartney were now producing music for a whole new audience—hip, culturally aware young people, no longer just screaming teenage girls. "Dr. Robert" was an in-joke reference to the physician who had given an unknowing George and John their first taste of LSD, while "Love You To" revealed George's burgeoning interest in Indian music. "Taxman," featuring a scorching raga-style solo from Paul, satirized the Labour government's tax policies. And John and Paul still found time to write one of the most popular children's songs of all time, "Yellow Submarine," for Ringo to sing.

Revolver also saw the birth of the idea of an album as a coherent body of work, not just a selection of songs randomly thrown together. The world now readily accepts the idea of pop music as an art form, but *Revolver* was perhaps the first album by a pop group to be regarded as such. And with its release, The Beatles took pop music into uncharted territory.

In spite of the album's experimentation, there were still more than enough fans to take *Revolver* straight to the number 1 spot, both in Britain and the United States. It went on to sell well over 2 million copies during that year and its reputation continues to grow with time. As new generations discover The Beatles, it is most often *Revolver* to which they respond most warmly. Indeed, in 1995, readers of British music magazine *Q* voted it the best album ever made; many who voted were not even born when the album was released.

John and George take time out from recording at Abbey Road to pose for the cameras, May 1966.

End of the road

The summer of 1966 saw The Beatles give their last paid public performances. Although by now Brian Epstein had realized that they had increasingly little interest in touring, he nevertheless committed them to a series of concerts around the world. Among these were the band's only dates in East Asia.

The reaction from their Japanese fans came as quite a shock to all four Beatles—they experienced something approaching delayed Beatlemania there. They were greeted at Tokyo airport by 1,500 ecstatic fans, but were shocked at the heavy-handed treatment meted out by a Japanese police force unused to such wild behavior from their teenagers. A total of 35,000 security guards were employed throughout The Beatles' three-day trip. Each of their shows at the Nippon Budokan was attended by an audience of 10,000 fans, and manned by 3,000 police officers. Throughout their stay in Japan, The Beatles were "imprisoned" in their luxury suite at the Tokyo Hilton. Armed police guards stood by every possible entrance. Bad though it was, there was worse to come.

On Sunday, July 3, The Beatles flew on to play two shows in Manila, the capital city of the Philippines. Newspapers widely reported that President Ferdinand Marcos and his family were to be guests of honor at the concerts, and that The Beatles would be invited to their palace the following morning. Unfortunately, nobody had informed the group of these arrangements. When a government official arrived at The Beatles' hotel to pick them up, he was told by Brian Epstein that they were sleeping and that under no circumstances could they be disturbed. This was reported by the local media as a deliberate snub. Chaos ensued. Both The Beatles' hotel and the British Embassy were inundated with bomb threats. In trying to leave the country, The Beatles' entourage faced every form of delay that petty bureaucracy could conceive. When the controversy first broke, President Marcos had all official security withdrawn and as The Beatles made their way through the airport to board their plane, they were kicked, spat at, and jostled by angry Filipinos. In retrospect, the violence of the reaction and the condemnation of the group in the local press may not have been entirely unconnected with the fact that Marcos was a ruthless dictator. It would be an unwise subject indeed who failed to rally to the flag under such circumstances.

Compared to the Philippines, the U.S. tour that took place the following month was a breeze. But it was increasingly difficult for the band to find the enthusiasm to play their famous hits; they didn't even bother to rehearse for the tour. On August 29, at San Francisco's Candlestick Park, The Beatles shuffled off stage having played a 33-minute set to the usual ecstatic reaction. They would never set foot on another stage together again.

Back in the U.K. after their tour, John sounds off about the group's treatment in Manila, July 1966.

An actor's life

When The Beatles returned to London from the States in August 1966, everyone–Brian included–knew that from then on things were going to be different. With the highly acclaimed *Revolver* at the top of the charts, they decided to take a break from being Beatles. There were no plans to record any new material for at least three months.

John spent a lot of time away from the other members of the band, most of it at Kenwood with Cynthia and Julian. His wife observed a less strident manner about him following the end of the tour, and interpreted John's mood as contentment at winning the battle for The Beatles' future direction.

The chief Beatle was by no means idle throughout this period, though. In spite of his reservations about *Help!*, John had remained friends with the American director Richard Lester. With a break in his schedule, Lester offered John a role alongside Michael Crawford in his new film, *How I Won The War*. Although he had no illusions about his talents as an actor, John couldn't resist the idea of a solo film role: "I was flattered at being asked," he confessed later. "The ego needed feeding, with The Beatles at a kind of crossroads."

The film was a cynical antiwar black comedy set during World War II, a theme that appealed greatly to John. To play his character–Private Gripweed–John had to make a few significant changes to his appearance. His Beatle mop was shorn in the British military style and he adopted National Health "granny glasses." Although he did not keep the shorter hairstyle, the specs stayed with him, creating yet another Beatle-inspired fashion.

Shooting took place in Germany and Spain. John was alone most of the time, but broke with tradition when he invited Cynthia to stay. In early October, Ringo and his wife Maureen also flew out to Spain to visit him. But although the experience of acting without the other Beatles had been a novelty, John felt little enthusiasm for the project. "The thing I remember is Dick Lester had more fun than I did," he later commented.

After completing work on the film, John opted to try his hand at TV, appearing in Peter Cook and Dudley Moore's satirical sketch show *Not Only ... But Also*. Lennon was a good friend of Cook, and had already appeared on the show the previous year, reading excerpts from *In His Own Write*. This time he appeared in a comedy sketch as the concierge of a public convenience, still wearing his "granny glasses."

Opposite: A shorn, bespectacled John on location in Almeria, Spain, 1966.

Right: John joins Peter Cook (far left) in a sketch from *Not Only ... But Also*.

Let me take you down ...

The Beatles resumed business on Thursday, November 24, with George Martin at the controls in Studio Two of Abbey Road. They would spend much of the remainder of 1966 recording just one song. While on location with Richard Lester, John had written a song that harked back to his childhood. It was named after a Salvation Army children's home in Liverpool just around the corner from Aunt Mimi's house—Strawberry Field.

"Strawberry Fields Forever" was the most complex recording The Beatles had ever attempted and required George Martin to bring new techniques to his armory of production skills. The song was originally written as an acoustic ballad, but as its arrangement evolved, it took on a much heavier tone, reminiscent of bands that were emerging from San Francisco at the time, such as the Jefferson Airplane. After a break of a few weeks, and worried that the song may have moved too far away from his original idea, John suggested an alternative version and asked George Martin to come up with some orchestral arrangements.

Ultimately, John liked both finished versions and asked Martin if there was any way the two versions could be combined. Since the tuning and tempo of each track were slightly different the prospects of successfully "splicing" them together seemed remote. Nonetheless, when Martin's engineer Geoff Emerick tried he was amazed to find that by speeding up the first version and slowing down the second, both tuning and tempo matched perfectly.

"Strawberry Fields Forever" came out in February 1967 backed by another classic, "Penny Lane"—Paul McCartney's own paean to a part of Liverpool familiar to all four Beatles. Both songs were intended to be part of an ambitious album concept, linked by songs inspired by the band's childhood. However, under pressure from EMI to release a new single, the two tracks were plucked from the album sessions and released as a double A-sided single.

Critical acclaim for the two tracks was taken as evidence of The Beatles' astounding artistic development. Over the years, "Strawberry Fields Forever" has grown in stature, and for many it stands as the greatest seven-inch single ever produced. The group also recorded a short promotional film for both songs, an early video in effect, incorporating color negative images and backward-running film. The combination of music and visuals remains electrifying, concisely evoking the psychedelic era.

Ironically, in spite of the lofty pronouncements of the music literati, "Strawberry Fields Forever" became the first Beatles single in almost five years *not* to top the U.K. charts. It stalled at number 2, behind "Release Me," a schmaltzy ballad by cabaret singer Engelbert Humperdinck. In the States, however, Humperdinck's track stalled at number 4, while "Penny Lane" topped the charts; "Strawberry Fields Forever" reached number 8 separately.

A mustachioed John during filming for the "Strawberry Fields Forever" promo film, January 1967.

Sgt. Pepper

For the first four months of 1967, The Beatles worked solidly in Abbey Road's Studio Two. Throughout this time they meticulously crafted what is arguably the most influential album in the history of popular music—*Sgt. Pepper's Lonely Hearts Club Band*. The record was conclusive proof of a supremely confident group working at the peak of its creative powers.

Continuing The Beatles' desire to produce a cohesive body of music, *Sgt. Pepper* is a concept album of sorts. It was Paul McCartney who came up with the idea of creating a mythical band: "Why don't we make the whole album as though the Pepper band really existed, as though Sgt. Pepper was doing the record?" he suggested.

The album took a total of five months and 700 hours of studio time to record. It cost £25,000 (approximately $37,000)—an unprecedented figure by 1967 standards. But the music throughout reveals a complexity never before heard on a pop album. *Sgt. Pepper* was rapidly lauded as a new benchmark in modern music.

The high point of the album was the closing track, "A Day In The Life." Unlike many of The Beatles' songs over the previous years, this was a genuine Lennon/McCartney collaboration, with John writing the opening and closing sections, and Paul penning the segment in between. The first two parts were linked by a 40-piece orchestra playing, at John's request, "a sound building up from nothing to the end of the world."

As with *Revolver*, the Lennon and McCartney contributions are relatively easy to identify. John's lyrics, influenced by his heavy consumption of LSD, stumbled down an ever more oblique path. Both John and Paul were open to inspiration from any source, however unlikely. The words of "Being For The Benefit Of Mister Kite" were drawn almost verbatim from a poster that John found in an antiques shop, while "Lucy In The Sky With Diamonds" was inspired by a painting his son Julian brought home from school. Famously, the song's title was misinterpreted as a reference to LSD, an early example of both fans and critics scouring Beatles songs for hidden references or "clues." (The "help" in "With A Little Help From My Friends," a song John and Paul wrote for Ringo, was thought by some to be another reference to drugs.) Paul's contributions were more traditionally melodic offerings, such as "When I'm Sixty-Four" and the plaintive "She's Leaving Home," while George's "Within You, Without You" reflected his growing interest in all things Indian. The group's continuing desire to experiment with sound made huge demands on George Martin, but the results were central to the new genre of "psychedelic" music.

Often critical of his Beatles work, this was one album that John had few doubts about: "*Sgt. Pepper* is the one. It was a peak. Paul and I were definitely working together."

Psychedelic bandsmen: The Beatles as pictured on the inside cover of *Sgt. Pepper*.

Cultural leaders

Although the heady days of Beatlemania were long gone, The Beatles were now in a league of their own, and each new stage in their development was eagerly scrutinized by the popular press. Such was their cultural dominance in the mid-1960s that each new single and album was viewed as a landmark release, casting a shadow over the rest of the pop scene. What The Beatles did one month would be copied by thousands of other bands the next, even to the point where inferior cover versions of Beatle album tracks made the charts.

However, the reaction to *Sgt. Pepper*—by both public and critics—was unlike that inspired by any other record before. It was no surprise that it topped the charts all over the world, but the magnitude of its success amazed everyone. On its U.K. release it went straight to number 1 and stayed there for six long months. Even after it left the Top 30 almost a year later, it continued to make occasional reappearances. By the early 1980s, it had sold over 10 million copies worldwide. The publicity surrounding the album's release on CD in 1992, on its 25th anniversary, took it high into the charts all over again.

The critics were unanimous in their praise, declaring *Sgt. Pepper* to be a genuine work of art. *The Times Literary Supplement* called it "a barometer of our times," while in the U.S., *Newsweek*'s Jack Kroll went further, comparing the LP with T. S. Eliot's work—in his eyes, "A Day in the Life" was The Beatles' "Waste Land." Just as there are those who remember exactly what they were doing and where they were the day John F. Kennedy was assassinated or the day Elvis died, a whole generation can still remember the first time they heard the album. Indeed, henceforth an artist's best work would often be referred to as their "Sgt. Pepper."

Moreover, the album's impact wasn't limited to just the music, groundbreaking though it was. *Sgt. Pepper*'s sleeve has become a Pop Art classic, crammed with images of The Beatles' heroes and other cultural icons, including Bob Dylan, Lewis Carroll, Karl Marx, and Aleister Crowley. Even The Beatles' own waxwork dummies from Madame Tussaud's made an appearance. Designed by British Pop artist Peter Blake, the sleeve showed the real Fab Four festooned as psychedelic bandsmen, a reflection of the craze for Victoriana that swept through London in the mid- to late 1960s. The lyrics to each song were printed on the back of the album—another first for a rock release.

The Beatles had pulled off the coolest of tricks. They were the darlings of the middle-class media, their peers watched their every move, they were still loved by their original teenage pop audience, and their commercial tunes appealed to young and old alike. Meanwhile, acid-heads and stoners found an "underground" subtext to the music too. At the time of *Sgt. Pepper*'s release The Beatles had truly become all things to all people.

John at Brian Epstein's house in London, May 1967, for the launch of *Sgt. Pepper*.

Love is all you need

Sgt. Pepper dominated the charts the world over. However, the dust had barely settled before The Beatles were ready to make history all over again. The first worldwide satellite TV link-up, which took place during the summer of 1967, was a pivotal moment in communications technology and a special pageant, called *Our World*, was planned to celebrate the event. It was to be a six-hour live TV broadcast with 26 participating nations. The total simultaneous television audience would be 400 million, by far and away the largest ever reached. Each nation was invited to nominate its own cultural ambassadors to take part in this historic event. The Beatles were called upon to represent Great Britain.

Brian Epstein decided that it was the perfect forum for a new single to receive its world premiere. The song chosen—"All You Need Is Love"—was primarily John's work. It gave ample proof, were proof needed, that as the most famous group in the world, The Beatles now felt no artistic constraints whatsoever. John's composition was a ponderous, heavily orchestrated piece, the verses of which were played seven beats to the bar—unheard of in most popular music. That The Beatles managed to turn all of this into the greatest singalong anthem of the "Love Generation" is testament to their consummate skills as songsmiths.

On June 25, 1967, the broadcast took place as planned, with The Beatles singing "All You Need Is Love" live accompanied by a prerecorded backing tape. They were joined in the studio by other pop notables, including Mick Jagger, Keith Richard, Marianne Faithfull, and Eric Clapton. The single went straight to the number 1 spot and—appropriately—occupied the top of the charts throughout what is now fondly remembered as the "Summer of Love."

By mid-1967 the "flower power" era had peaked. What began spontaneously in San Francisco's Haight-Ashbury district a few years earlier was now a worldwide phenomenon. However, "Love and Peace" became more a fashionable slogan than the heralding of a radical new lifestyle. "All You Need Is Love" gave hippies a certain amount of cultural legitimacy. During that summer it seemed that everyone was growing their hair, dressing in swirling psychedelic colors, and sporting flowers, beads, and bells.

Ultimately it was not a revolution; it was just another fad. But for many who lived through the time—even those with no great interest in music—"All You Need Is Love" will be remembered as a song that all but defined the high-water mark of 1960s optimism.

Opposite: John's "All You Need Is Love" became a 1960s anthem.
Right: The Beatles promote their single for the "Summer of Love" at Abbey Road Studios, June 25, 1967.

Meeting the Maharishi

Although his efforts as a songwriter were overshadowed by Lennon and McCartney, The Beatles' lead guitarist George Harrison had been slowly developing his own songwriting talents in the background. (His first solo Beatles composition—"Don't Bother Me"—was on their 1963 album *With The Beatles*.) During 1965, just before the recording of *Rubber Soul*, George had acquired a sitar—a traditional Indian stringed instrument—signaling what would be a lengthy infatuation with all things Asian. George had first used the instrument to play the solo on John's "Norwegian Wood." Thereafter he had taken lessons and befriended the sitar virtuoso Ravi Shankar. This developed into a genuine love and understanding of Indian music that colored George's contributions to *Rubber Soul, Revolver*, and *Sgt. Pepper*.

During April 1967, George's wife Pattie had noticed a poster announcing a public lecture featuring the Maharishi Mahesh Yogi. The Harrisons and their friends had already become intrigued by Transcendental Meditation. At Pattie's request George persuaded the other Beatles to join them at the lecture. John in particular was keen to know more about it.

Thus it was that on Thursday, April 24, The Beatles joined a small crowd at the Hilton Hotel, in London's Park Lane. There they watched and heard a middle-aged, bearded, long-haired Indian gentleman wearing only a robe describe, in a high-pitched voice, how a person could achieve true inner peace through the practice of meditation. It was a message that John, with his increasingly turbulent life, was all too ready to take on board. After the lecture, The Beatles sent word that they would like a private meeting with the Maharishi. Clearly such high-profile disciples could not be turned away. The Beatles were invited to join the Maharishi on a course of indoctrination at University College, Bangor, on the coast of North Wales. The Beatles asked Brian Epstein if he would like to join them but, as he had already made other plans, he said no.

The media noted this exotic and strange new direction that The Beatles were taking, and were out in force to see the group and their entourage—including Pattie Harrison, actress Jane Asher (then dating Paul McCartney), Mick Jagger, and his girlfriend singer Marianne Faithfull—leaving on a specially chartered train from Paddington station, west London. But Cynthia Lennon missed the train—she was held back by a policeman who thought she was one of the many fans who had joined the crowd to see off the group. Cynthia eventually made her own way to Bangor, but the incident seemed somehow symbolic of the growing distance between herself and her husband, who increasingly seemed to be heading for places where she couldn't follow.

Followers of the Maharishi: The Beatles at the Bangor seminar weekend, August 1967.

Roll up ...

The Beatles' next project was to be a TV musical, *Magical Mystery Tour*. However, after the triumph of *Sgt. Pepper*, it was to give the band's collective ego a sizable dent. Following Brian's death, The Beatles opted to manage their own affairs, and although John was still popularly perceived as the "leader" of The Beatles, Paul now began to assert himself with increasing authority. He launched himself enthusiastically into the project—the group were to write, produce, direct, star in, score, and edit the film themselves.

The difficulties started immediately. The Beatles decided to hire the famous Shepperton Studios, but didn't realize it had to be booked months in advance. For the storyline, Paul had an idea inspired by West Coast legend Ken Kesey who, two years earlier, had attracted notoriety by taking a bus troupe of assorted oddballs on an LSD-soaked tour of California. In the hands of four working-class Liverpool lads, this became an outing through the English countryside in a bus populated by sideshow freaks and music-hall renegades. Paul's plan was that the plot would effectively generate itself as they drove along.

So The Beatles hired a luxury bus, selected actors from agency directories, and set off to make a film. It all sounded so easy. With no itinerary planned, the bus would go wherever any Beatle wanted it to go. In the event, however, the filming was a catastrophe. The group gave little thought to the mayhem that might be caused to other road users when the bus ambled along tiny country lanes creating traffic jams, or at the end of a day's filming when nobody had remembered to book a hotel for the large entourage. Brian certainly wouldn't have let such things happen.

At the end of their mystery tour, The Beatles had over 10 hours of material and booked an editing suite for one week to put the film together. In the end it took 11 weeks to create a one-hour show, broadcast by the BBC on December 26, 1967. About 15 million viewers tuned in for what many had hoped would be a visual equivalent to *Sgt. Pepper*. Most were disappointed. Matters had not been helped by the fact that although the film had been made in color, the BBC broadcast it in black and white. The following day the British press gave the film a unanimous thumbs-down—one dismissing it as "blatant rubbish."

Magical Mystery Tour was largely Paul's work. John was not wholly behind the project: "George and I were sort of grumbling about the fuckin' movie and we thought we'd better do it and we had the feeling that we owed it to the public to do these things," he later grouched. For his part, the ever-optimistic Paul has always remained unapologetic about *Magical Mystery Tour*: "I think it was a good show. It will have its day, you know."

"I am the eggman ..."—John filming *Magical Mystery Tour,* September 1967. His famous psychedelic Rolls-Royce is visible in the background.

Apple Corps

By Beatle standards, *Magical Mystery Tour* had been a failure. However, still impervious to the need for outside management, The Beatles decided to push their entrepreneurial flair to the limit. The next move would see the birth of The Beatles as alternative businessmen.

In December 1967, The Beatles gave two young Dutch designers £100,000 (approximately $150,000) to open up a clothes store. Known collectively as The Fool, Simon Posthuma and Marijka Koger had worked almost exclusively for The Beatles for the past year, designing their clothes, their home interiors, and even the psychedelic patterning for John's Rolls-Royce.

Located on a corner in a four-story house at 94 Baker Street, London, the Apple Boutique was to be "a beautiful place where you could buy beautiful things." This was only the start. The Beatles aimed to create a new type of business empire of which *they* were in control.

The boutique was to be followed by other exciting new projects such as Apple Electronics, Apple Records, Apple Films, Apple Music, and Apple Books. The whole operation came under the umbrella Apple Corps Ltd. Based in a five-story Georgian building in the heart of London's Mayfair, 3 Savile Row would become headquarters for one of the most absurdly unsuccessful business ventures of the 1960s. Nevertheless, it's perhaps worth remembering that the idea was one clearly born out of the skyscraping optimism of that decade and represented a heartfelt desire to encourage creative artists.

Perhaps the most extreme development was the birth of the Apple Foundation for the Arts —as Paul put it: "We're in a happy position of not needing any more money so for the first time the bosses are not in it for the profit. If you come to me and say 'I've had such and such a dream,' I'll say to you, 'Go away and do it.'" Predictably, the Foundation was immediately overwhelmed with every type of business proposal imaginable, most of them unworkable.

With the exception of the record label, which enjoyed considerable success, by the end of 1968 every other aspect of Apple's activities had shed a small fortune. Apple Films and Apple Books had yet to come up with a single product; in spite of the heavy subsidy, Apple Electronics looked incapable of manufacturing a viable product.

One by one, the failing divisions folded. When the boutique closed, some seven months after its opening, Paul simply told the press: "The Beatles are tired of being shopkeepers." One evening, The Beatles and their families visited the store and helped themselves to anything they wanted. The following day they announced that everyone else could do the same. (Ironically, the boutique had been plagued by shoplifting and many people had been doing exactly that for some time.) Hundreds of shoppers, held in check by a dozen policemen, stormed the doors and made off with anything they could lay their hands on.

Beatles in the high street—the Apple Boutique brought psychedelia to central London.

Meditative times

The time The Beatles had spent with the Maharishi had provided them with a valuable recuperative retreat from the pressures of being the world's most famous pop stars. February 1968 saw them embark on what was intended to be a three-month period studying meditation at the Maharishi's Indian ashram in Rishikesh, overlooking the River Ganges. The Maharishi lived in the relative luxury of a fenced compound. The Beatles, their wives, and girlfriends were accompanied by a selection of fellow celebrities in search of enlightenment, including The Beach Boys' Mike Love, actress Mia Farrow, and the U.K. pop star Donovan.

The intensive religious tuition and chanting sessions, combined with the restrictive diets, proved a testing time for people used to life's luxuries. Ringo, who had been more than a little cynical even at the start of the episode, was the first to crack. He and his wife Maureen made their exit after only 10 days, claiming they had eaten enough of the spicy vegetarian food (they had allegedly taken a large supply of Heinz baked beans with them). A month later Paul McCartney and Jane Asher also made their excuses and left.

John and George stayed on, although they gradually started to become suspicious about their host. It was rumored that the Maharishi's interest in Mia Farrow was rather more physical than might be expected of a guru. Somewhat bitterly, they also decided to leave. It's worth noting that the remaining two Beatles departed Rishikesh without giving the Maharishi the chance to deny the accusations of misconduct or to defend himself. Certainly, he had never stipulated that he was sexually abstinent. Moreover, hindsight suggests that at least one member of The Beatles' entourage may have engineered the rumors in the first place to prevent the Maharishi from becoming too influential with the Fab Four.

It seemed that, like the Apple Boutique, the Maharishi was simply another new toy that The Beatles had grown bored of and were now throwing away. The media had a field day when the news broke. The Beatles themselves were offhand about the episode. "We made a mistake," Paul told the press. "We thought there was more to him than there was. He's human. We thought at first that he wasn't." Although the trip to India could have been looked upon as a public humiliation, John always viewed it in a positive light. The new environment had helped him come through what had become an escalating dependency on certain drugs. Moreover, he had returned from Rishikesh with over 20 new songs, many of which would find their way onto The Beatles' new album. One of them was written about the Maharishi, although, in John's own words, he "copped out" and changed all the direct references to the holy man. The world would hear the song as "Sexy Sadie."

The Indian trip, March 1968. Left to right: Pattie Harrison, John Lennon, Mike Love, the Maharishi, George Harrison, Mia Farrow, Donovan, Paul McCartney, Jane Asher, and Cynthia Lennon.

4 The Dream Is Over

Although their artistic triumphs continue, the four Beatles become increasingly isolated from one another as the decade draws to a close. John has apparently lost interest in the band he created and is increasingly following his own direction. Along with his new wife, Yoko Ono, he takes the first tentative steps along what will be an eccentric solo path. The end of the decade sees John making news headlines because of his prominent peace campaigns rather than for his music.

John and Yoko

Nineteen sixty-eight was to be a turbulent year for both John Lennon and The Beatles. Over the previous year John's relationship with his wife Cynthia had become increasingly strained and they struggled to find common ground. Moreover, his private life was soon to be thrust into the public arena due to the appearance of Japanese artist Yoko Ono. It was a relationship that one way or another would last the rest of his life.

John had always been the Beatle most open to experimentation. He had wholeheartedly embraced marijuana, and had become a frequent user of LSD by the beginning of 1966. This thirst for novelty also saw a burgeoning interest in the world of avant-garde art. It was while attending an exhibition at London's Indica Gallery in November 1966 that John first encountered Yoko Ono, the show's featured artist. He was immediately intrigued. Yoko's work was confident and provocative. For one of her exhibits she asked John to climb a ladder and hammer an imaginary nail into a wall. This, she said, would cost him five shillings. Slightly bemused, John dryly replied "I'll give you an imaginary five shillings." The connection was made. John would later say of the meeting:

"Imagine two cars of the same make heading towards each other and they're gonna crash head-on ... they're doing a hundred miles an hour ... they both slam their brakes on ... and they stop just in the nick of time, with their bumpers almost touching. That's what it was like from the moment I first met her ... I had no doubt I'd met The One."

Cynthia had always known that John was no saint when it came to fending off advances from the many groupies inevitably drawn to the world's most famous pop group. But she took faith in the fact that it was always to her that he would return, commenting later: "Whatever John did outside our marriage, he didn't flaunt anything." But John's honesty could sometimes be brutal. On one occasion he casually told her: "I want to get it off my chest, Cyn. There have been hundreds of other women."

In the middle of May 1968, with Cynthia away on holiday, John invited Yoko to his Surrey home, supposedly to work on a series of sound collages. From that day onward John and Yoko became virtually inseparable. The other three Beatles had seen nothing like it before: their private and working lives had always been totally separate—no one had ever managed to break their way into a Beatle's creative life. John and Yoko's affair moved at a rapid pace. On November 8, 1968, following acrimonious legal wrangling, Cynthia was awarded a decree nisi divorce on the grounds of her husband's adultery.

Early in 1969, John sold Kenwood, his home of the past five years. He and Yoko moved into Tittenhurst Park, a secluded mansion near the town of Ascot in Berkshire.

John and Yoko at John's first proper art exhibition, *You Are Here*, July 1968.

Crises and cartoons

From the moment John and Yoko became an item, Yoko's influence made itself felt, even spreading into the heart of The Beatles' most hallowed territory—the recording studio. In the past, wives and girlfriends had often visited The Beatles while they were recording at Abbey Road, but they were invariably kept at a distance from the creative decision making. When Yoko appeared, all that changed. Although John attended all the sessions, made suggestions, and played his guitar as he had always done, now he had a constant companion at his side, whispering into his ear. From that point onward, Yoko was always present, a sounding-board for John's music-making.

The recording sessions for the next album were accompanied by a great deal of bad feeling. Yoko's presence certainly affected the studio atmosphere between the four musicians, but at the same time Paul McCartney now began to assert his own "leadership" of the group, often in a heavy-handed way. On August 20, Ringo walked out on the band for two weeks after Paul criticized his playing. Paul, now more than competent on most instruments, took over the drumming in his absence. When Ringo returned, he found that the others had covered his drums with flowers to welcome him back. However, Ringo wasn't the only Beatle to feel he was being talked down to. Things were similarly fractious between Paul and George, who felt that Paul was all too often trying to tell him how he should play his guitar. Only John seemed oblivious to all of this bad feeling.

The year 1968 also saw the conclusion of a project that had been hanging around for nearly two years—a Beatles animation film. The band all hated the idea at the time—possibly because they had disliked the U.S. Beatles cartoon series, which had been handled by the same producer, Al Brodax. The film was a contractual obligation to United Artists as far as The Beatles were concerned, and they deliberately had very little involvement in it, agreeing only to supplying four new songs and a live-action sequence for the ending. In spite of this, the end result, *Yellow Submarine*, was something of a cinematic triumph. The psychedelic style of animation perfectly captured the mood of the late 1960s while the story, crafted from lyrics and characters in songs from the *Rubber Soul*, *Revolver*, and *Sgt. Pepper* albums, was entertaining and surprisingly coherent. The finished film was a visually stimulating cartoon for children that also had a foot in the "underground" subculture of the decade—a sort of *Alice In Wonderland* for the 1960s.

The Beatles attended the premiere of the film, on July 17 at the London Pavilion cinema in Piccadilly Circus. John used the opportunity to make his first high-profile public appearance with Yoko Ono at his side.

Still smiling, John, George, and Paul work on their new album at Abbey Road Studios, 1968.

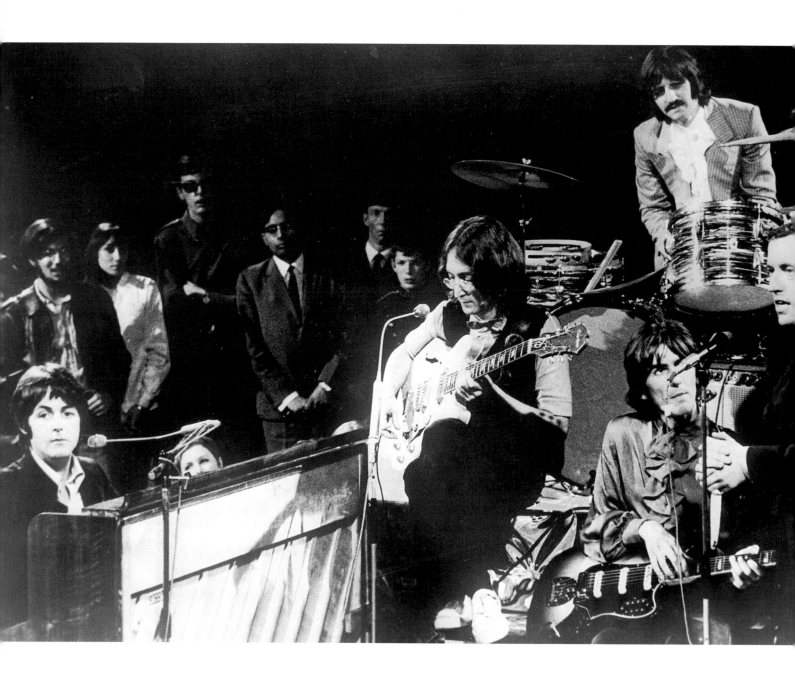

The White Album

From May until October of 1968, The Beatles worked solidly in the studio. Sometimes they worked in several studios at the same time. Although the band played together on most of the backing tracks, it was invariably the composer who added the finishing touches to his own song. Many of the songs were strikingly simple and based around acoustic guitars—most had been written in this way while The Beatles were sitting around the ashram in Rishikesh. The jacket, too, was about as basic as it could be—a plain white gatefold—in marked contrast to the dense, colorful sleeve of their previous LP, *Sgt. Pepper*. The album's official title was simply *The Beatles*, though it soon became known popularly as *The White Album*.

For all their personal differences, the recording sessions yielded well over 30 new songs, providing the group with two complete albums' worth of new material. Producer George Martin wanted the material pared down to the 14 best songs, but The Beatles remained convinced that the work was good enough to be released as a double album set.

Given the spirit in which it was made, *The White Album* is certainly the most fascinating of The Beatles' collections. Indeed, there are many who rate it as their best work, among them John Lennon: "it was our first unselfconscious album ... I always preferred the double album because *my* music is better on that album."

Among the album's high points were John's "Glass Onion"—a song aimed at the critics and fans who read unintended meanings into his songs. The album also featured one of his personal favorites, "Happiness Is A Warm Gun." It was interpreted by some as being about heroin—which John was now regularly using—although he refuted the idea: "I think it's a beautiful song. I like all the different things that are happening. It wasn't about 'H' at all."

Another significant track is John's "Revolution 9," a disturbing eight-minute sound collage assembled by himself and Yoko. John had wanted it released as a single; the other three Beatles had been opposed to it even appearing on the album. According to John: "It was an unconscious picture of what I actually think will happen ... like a drawing of revolution. All the thing was made with loops. I had about 30 loops going, fed them into one basic track ... chopping it up, making it backwards ... Number 9 turned out to be my birthday and my lucky number. There are many symbolic things about it, but it just happened you know ... I was just using all the bits to make a montage. I really wanted that released."

When it was released in October 1968, *The White Album* became the fastest-selling album up to that date, going on to sell almost 10 million copies throughout the world.

During September 1968, The Beatles took time out from their sessions for *The White Album* and appeared on David Frost's TV show to premiere their new single, "Hey Jude." In fact, the song was originally titled "Hey Jules," and was written by Paul McCartney for John's son Julian.

Get Back

With John's attentions firmly sidelined, Paul McCartney was now the motivating force behind The Beatles. Concerned at the apparent apathy of the others, he felt they needed something on which they could focus. He came up with the idea of turning the rehearsals and recordings for their next album into a television documentary, the climax of which would be a one-off live performance.

The taped rehearsals started in January 1969, but tensions were apparent from the start. These were partly due to the fact that Yoko was always there with John. The real problem, though, was that Paul seemed to be the only Beatle who *really* wanted to be there at all. His annoyance at the antipathy surrounding him spilled over into arguments about playing. Equally, the other three were clearly beginning to tire of Paul's assertiveness. On January 10, George walked out—in addition to his difficulties with Paul, John had criticized his songwriting two days before, and George had simply had enough of it.

The idea for the new album—still unnamed, but with a working title of "Get Back"—was to capture a spontaneous live recording. The sessions were scheduled to take place at the new Apple Studios in the basement of The Beatles' Savile Row office. However, when the group turned up to start work they found chaos. The studio—designed by Apple's in-house boffin whom John had dubbed "Magic Alex"—resembled a home-built electronics laboratory with dozens of tiny loudspeakers placed all around the studio. The briefest of test recordings proved that the new environment would be useless for The Beatles' needs. The next week was spent undoing Magic Alex's handiwork and bringing in equipment from Abbey Road.

Meanwhile, another problem emerged. New songs were taking longer than anticipated to develop, and it was becoming clear that the budget for filming The Beatles' performance couldn't stretch through the recording of the album, which looked as though it might last up to six months. So it was decided that The Beatles would perform an unannounced concert on the roof of their Savile Row headquarters, which would be filmed.

On Thursday, January 30, 1969, The Beatles took to an impromptu stage at the top of the building, surrounded by family, friends, and film crews. As they struck up the opening chords to "Get Back," local office workers came out to investigate the noise. Gradually, the narrow roads around Mayfair in central London became congested, and the police arrived. After 42 minutes of playing, and distracted by the number of police officers who were by now trying to get them to stop, The Beatles ended the show with another version of "Get Back." With the guitar chords fading, John quipped: "I'd like to say thank you on behalf of the group and ourselves and I hope we passed the audition." The Beatles' final public performance was over.

The end—The Beatles perform a free concert on the roof of the Apple office, January 30, 1969.

Experiments in the avant-garde

Sgt. Pepper represented both the peak of John and Paul's partnership and the last time that the two were to collaborate closely. Yoko Ono effectively took over as John's creative partner from the start of their relationship in 1968. Under her influence, John felt encouraged to indulge his growing interests in alternative or experimental art forms. As a conceptual artist, Yoko taught John that an idea could be more important than a tangible artifact, such as a song or a record. Or, as John put it, "She encouraged the freak in me."

Paul McCartney was at close hand to see Yoko's impact on his friend:

"Once he met Yoko ... he let out all these bizarre sides to his character. He didn't dare do it when he was living in suburbia with Cynthia."

"Yoko would say 'This is very good art, we must do this' and she gave him the freedom to do it. In fact she wanted more: 'Do it double. Be more daring. Take all your clothes off.' She always pushed him, which he liked. Nobody had ever pushed him before."

John and Yoko's first collaboration had been *Unfinished Music No. 1–Two Virgins*, which was recorded and released in 1968. A series of sound collages in a similar vein to "Revolution 9," the music aroused little consumer interest. Few regular Beatles fans would have even considered it to be music at all. The sleeve, however, did create some notoriety—it was a full-frontal nude photograph of John and Yoko. Eventually, the album was made available only in a brown paper bag. Surprisingly, given the huge popularity of The Beatles, if not the uncompromising music, the album only sold around 5,000 copies in Britain on release.

The following year, the duo recorded a similar album, *Unfinished Music No. 2–Life With The Lions*, released on Apple's experimental offshoot label, Zapple, but this one too met with public indifference. One side of the album was recorded on a cassette during Yoko's failed pregnancy at Queen Charlotte Hospital. The flip side featured music from a set that the two had performed during an avant-garde musical evening at Cambridge University on March 2, 1969. Again, the confrontational material failed to attract much interest.

Such esoteric activities cut little ice with The Beatles' traditional fans, many of whom saw Yoko as a corrupting interloper or gold digger. Few realized that she actually came from a background of wealth and privilege, and had little need of a share in John's fortune. Nonetheless, many people felt that it was Yoko Ono who was directly responsible for breaking up The Beatles. And to Beatles fans, that was an unforgivable sin.

Yoko and John performed a set of free-form, avant-garde material at Cambridge University in 1969.

John Ono Lennon

When John Lennon and Yoko Ono first became involved with each other, they were both married to other partners. After an acrimonious six months, Cynthia divorced John in November 1968. Three months later, Yoko was divorced from her estranged husband, the American jazz musician and film producer Anthony Cox.

By stark contrast to John's childhood, Yoko Ono was born into luxury. Her father Eisuke Ono was president of a Japanese bank in San Francisco, while her mother was from an aristocratic family that could lay claim to being one of the wealthiest in Japan. Yoko grew up in an environment of maids and private tutors; money was never a cause for concern.

At the age of 18 Yoko dropped out of New York's prestigious Sarah Lawrence College to elope with her first husband, Toshi Ichiyanagi. Together they immersed themselves in the burgeoning avant-garde art scene. However, Yoko's early efforts met largely with apathy until she met up with Anthony Cox. Together they formed a formidable duo and it was during this time that Yoko learned the art and importance of self-publicity. She made her first appearances as an experimental artist in London in 1962 and over the years preceding her first encounter with John Lennon, she became known as a cutting-edge artist.

Although Yoko's association with John made her well known outside of the art world, her work was never treated with respect beyond her own circle. This was a source of great annoyance to John and, he claimed, a major factor in his eventual decision to abandon his home country: "She's a serious artist, you know!"

Above (top half): The marriage certificate—it was John's second wedding, and Yoko's third.

Yoko's relationship with Anthony Cox had evidently always been a difficult one, and although highly productive in artistic terms, it was never destined to be long-lasting. Yoko had little difficulty getting a divorce when she realized that she wanted to spend her future with John, although problems were later to arise over whether she or Cox were to have custody of their daughter, Kyoko.

On March 20, 1969, John and Yoko took a flight from Paris to Gibraltar where they were married by the Registrar at the British Consulate. They remained in Gibraltar for just 72 minutes before taking a return flight to Paris. One month later, after a discussion in which Yoko lightheartedly told John that she objected to the idea of having to take his surname, he symbolically changed his middle name by deed poll from Winston to Ono. Clearly, in his own mind, John Lennon was entering a new phase in his life.

John and Yoko on their wedding day—March 20, 1969—in front of the Rock of Gibraltar.

Giving peace a chance

"I've always been politically minded, you know, and against the status quo," John once commented. His stance had remained that of an outsider, whether as a teenage Teddy Boy or as the most unpredictable element in The Beatles. "It's pretty basic when you're brought up like I was, to hate and fear the police as a natural enemy and despise the army as something that takes everybody away and leaves them dead somewhere."

Even at the height of Beatlemania, John had always been prepared to speak his mind on political or moral issues. But by the end of the 1960s, having staged a succession of highly publicized propaganda stunts, John and Yoko had carved a role for themselves as the world's most prominent campaigners for peace.

Their first public gesture took place as early as June 1968 when they participated in the National Sculpture Exhibition in Coventry. They each planted an acorn in the grounds of the cathedral; one pointing to the east and one to the west, symbolizing the meeting of two cultures. For the occasion John coined the slogan "Plant an Acorn for Peace."

They stepped up their efforts in 1969 with a series of bizarre "Bed-ins" and offbeat attention-grabbing stunts such as concealing themselves within a giant bag—they called it "bagism." Inevitably, the stunts grabbed headlines and when interviewed about their latest act, John and Yoko would invariably bring the subject round to the need for peace. Their most famous event took place at the Queen Elizabeth Hotel, in Montreal, Canada. For 10 days the Lennons' suite became the centre of all manner of bizarre media activity. They enjoyed high-profile visits from supporters such as Dr. Timothy Leary, and attracted TV crews from all over the world. It was also the location they chose to record their first single—an anthem for their peace protest, "Give Peace A Chance." That it was crudely recorded and performed was not the point. In his mind, John was turning the tables on the media that had for so long fed on The Beatles. "Give Peace A Chance" was the first single attributed to John's new group—The Plastic Ono Band.

The single was an immediate success, and has since become the definitive peace anthem throughout the world. John certainly succeeded in his original aim for the song: "In my secret heart of hearts I wanted to write something that would take over from 'We Shall Overcome.'" He later admitted that "one of the biggest moments of my life" was when he saw a news program in which half a million anti-Vietnam War protesters were shown standing outside the White House singing his song.

Opposite: The Lennons bed down for peace in the Amsterdam Hilton, March, 1969.

Right: It's in the bag—John and Yoko on the U.K.'s *Today* program, April 1, 1969.

Introducing Mr. Klein

Although The Beatles were still best-selling artists, their business affairs had been spiraling out of control since the death of Brian Epstein. No one had taken control of Apple, and despite The Beatles' healthy record sales, the company had been losing money for some time. The group were desperately in need of new management.

There was no shortage of offers to take up the mantle. Ultimately, it was Allen Klein, America's premier showbiz lawyer, who halted the decline of the Apple business empire. The Beatles had first been told about Klein by Mick Jagger in 1966. Although The Rolling Stones—for whom Klein had been employed as a business adviser—sold far fewer records than The Beatles, they were making considerably more money.

Klein had publicly expressed an interest in representing The Beatles on several previous occasions after Brian Epstein's death, but at that time they had been keen to handle their own affairs. However, by early 1969, with a small fortune leaking out of Apple, it was John who took the initiative and arranged a meeting with Klein. Impressed by the fact that the lawyer knew his songs, and wasn't a "suit" like the other businessmen he'd come across, John convinced George and Ringo that Klein should represent them.

However, this decision was a difficult one for Paul McCartney. He was currently engaged to New York photographer Linda Eastman, whose father Lee Eastman was also a well-respected entertainment lawyer. Paul wanted Eastman's firm to represent The Beatles. The scene was set for the first serous rift in the band's ranks. At an Apple board meeting, Paul McCartney was outvoted by three to one. But Paul stood his ground. Although Allen Klein was now in control of Apple, Paul hired Eastman to manage his own personal affairs.

An uneasy alliance was now in place, though it seemed unlikely to hold for long. At every possible crossroads the interests of Paul and the others now seemed to be at odds. These irreconcilable differences would ultimately provide the spark for the demise of the Fab Four.

In the meantime, Allen Klein ruthlessly set about clearing up the aftermath of the Apple debacle. Any activity not directly related to The Beatles or their music was terminated, and many members of the Apple staff were sacked. Later, with his customary honesty, John more or less wrote off The Beatles' attempt at "Western Communism":

"Apple was a manifestation of Beatle naivete, collective naivete," he admitted. "We really didn't get approached by the best artists in the world ... we got all the ones who everyone had thrown out." The Beatles had failed as enlightened businessmen and seemed to have stopped caring about the one thing that had made them great in the first place: their music.

Hard-nosed showbiz lawyer Allen Klein (far left) stepped in to sort out Apple's problems in 1969. Klein had the backing of John, George, and Ringo, but Paul McCartney stood firm against him.

One more time

After having spent much of February trying to finish off the "Get Back" project, the band's enthusiasm for the album had begun to wane. They decided to hand over their backing tapes to producer Glyn Johns. As John remembered, interest in the project was at an all-time low: "We didn't want to know about it anymore, so we just left it and said 'Here, mix it' ... Nobody called anybody about it, and the tapes were left there."

The results were not impressive. Twenty-nine hours of music had been mixed down to a single album. The Beatles had wanted the album to sound spontaneous, but the tapes from the sessions merely sounded rough. John was still keen for the LP to be released as it stood: "I didn't care. I thought it was good to let it out and show people what had happened to us ... 'We don't play together anymore, you know, leave us alone.'" He was voted down by the others. They decided to put the project on the shelf for a while.

Then, in June 1969, Paul McCartney contacted George Martin with an unexpected request. He said that The Beatles wanted to record an album with him again, just as they had on previous highlights such as *Revolver* and *Sgt. Pepper*. For the first three weeks of July, they block-booked Abbey Road Studios. Miraculously, all four Beatles managed to put their personal differences behind them to concentrate on recording together again.

The resulting album was named after the home of all of their classic recordings—*Abbey Road*. Seized upon by fans and critics alike as undeniable proof that The Beatles were still a viable working group, the album sold in phenomenal quantities, even by Beatle standards. It went straight to number 1 in the U.K., and did not budge from the top spot for the next five months. To date, it has now sold over 10 million copies worldwide.

Abbey Road showed that despite having already recorded many of the benchmark singles and albums of the 1960s, The Beatles were still developing as musicians and songwriters. George Harrison, who had always struggled hard to have his own songs included on Beatles albums, penned two of the LP's most beautiful and striking songs—"Something" and "Here Comes The Sun." Side two of the record was mostly devoted to a superb medley masterminded by Paul, but John provided the raunchy "Come Together" and the extraordinary bluesy workout "I Want You (She's So Heavy)," a stark declaration of love for Yoko that ended with a grim repetitive riff and squalls of white noise.

The high standard of *Abbey Road* led many to believe that The Beatles were capable of dominating the forthcoming decade every bit as decisively as they had the 1960s—a period they had all but defined. Instead, it was to be their final gift to the world, an against-all-odds triumph by four men who by now really had given all they had to give as a group.

Smiles for the camera: The Beatles pull together one last time for *Abbey Road*.

Plastic Ono Band

By the time The Beatles were recording *Abbey Road*, John had already decided that he'd had enough. He wanted to put the Fab Four behind him and "leave all that for The Monkees," as he told *Melody Maker* music paper. His interests now lay in the idea of The Plastic Ono Band. He envisaged his new project as being the complete antithesis of The Beatles. He wanted to record swiftly and spontaneously, and have the results in the shops as quickly as possible. The idea drew inspiration from his new partner's avant-garde sensibilities:

"Plastic Ono Band was a concept of Yoko's," he told the press, "an imaginary band ... some pieces of plastic and a tape recorder ... her idea was a completely robot pop group ... there's nobody in the band."

John and Yoko only ever got round to making some miniature plasticine models, and in practice The Plastic Ono Band became a loose pool of musician friends who would sometimes also include George Harrison and Ringo Starr. The band was kick started when John and Yoko offered to perform at a rock concert in Toronto in September 1969. John literally put a band together overnight, comprising himself and Yoko, session drummer Andy White, Eric Clapton on guitar, and Klaus Voormann—a friend from the Hamburg days—on bass. They rehearsed a set, predominantly made up of old rock-and-roll standards, on the flight to Canada the day before the concert. On stage, the music was rough and ready. The critics were not that impressed, but the spontaneity of the performance was perfectly in line with John's new ideas. The event was documented on the album *Live Peace In Toronto 1969*.

Back in England, John continued his peace campaign with one of his most controversial stunts. Always uncomfortable with the "honor" of having been awarded the MBE, he took the decision to return it, on November 25, 1969, as a way of publicly protesting about British foreign policy. In the letter that accompanied his medal, he told Her Majesty the Queen: "I am returning my MBE in protest at Britain's involvement in the Nigeria-Biafra thing [and] against our support of America in Vietnam." Immediately there was an outraged reaction from the British Establishment, the very people who had protested when The Beatles were awarded their MBEs back in 1965. John's Aunt Mimi, with whom he'd left the medal, was also furious: "Over my dead body would I have given you that medal to insult the Queen with," she raged, later admitting, "He broke my heart over that." In fact, in an audaciously irreverent gesture, Lennon added a further reason for returning the medal: as a protest against his latest single, "Cold Turkey," slipping down the charts.

Toward the end of the 1960s, Yoko replaced Paul McCartney as John's musical collaborator.

Primal screaming

By 1969 John Lennon's relationship with Yoko Ono had become pivotal to his entire existence. But away from Yoko, John had a number of problems to resolve. Not least of these was his escalating use of heroin. "Cold Turkey"—The Plastic Ono Band's second single—was a powerfully harrowing document of his ongoing battle to kick the drug. The single was awash with disturbing moans and screams from John; Ringo played drums on the track, and sometime Plastic Ono Band member Eric Clapton contributed searing guitar lines. John had been naturally drawn to experiment with drugs, but had always felt in control of them until he started to take heroin. He was disturbed to find that unlike the other substances he'd indulged in, heroin was a drug that was difficult to give up.

From the start of their relationship, John and Yoko had decided that although they each had a child from a previous marriage, they also wanted one together. In August 1969, when Yoko became pregnant, John decided it would be a good time to get himself "clean." Fearing the adverse publicity that would accompany any revelations that he was being treated in a hospital or clinic, he attempted to end his addiction himself, as suddenly and completely as possible. Such an abrupt termination of heroin use results in certain distinct side effects— clammy skin and periodic outbreaks of gooseflesh. For this reason the treatment is sometimes known as "cold turkey." However, this time around John's resolve failed. In October, Yoko was rushed to hospital where she miscarried. Hurt and bitterly disappointed at another failed pregnancy, John started using heroin once more.

Refuge of a sort came in an unlikely form. That same year, John read the book *The Primal Scream (Primal Therapy: The Cure For Neurosis)*, written by Californian psychiatrist Dr. Arthur Janov. The principles of primal scream therapy work on the assumption that every person has a series of defenses that when stripped away reveal the individual as they truly are. According to Janov, every personal issue or problem that an individual faces can be isolated and overcome through an often intense dialog—i.e., they can quite literally be "screamed away." In John's case, many of his psychological problems were linked to his difficult childhood—the death of his mother and the absence of his father from an early age. In April 1970, John and Yoko flew to the U.S. to undergo four months of primal therapy. It was a cathartic experience that resulted in an increase in John's self-awareness and helped him lay to rest some of the demons that had plagued him throughout his life.

The therapy didn't help him end his drug problems—they would linger for some time. But it was an important inspiration for the soul-baring that would characterize his songwriting over the next few years, in particular his 1970 album *John Lennon/Plastic Ono Band*.

Pop's ambassador for peace, looking distinctly Christlike, in 1969.

The end of the Fab Four

Although *Abbey Road* had been an artistic success, John had not found it a rewarding experience. Still keen to keep the band going, Paul proposed to get The Beatles back on stage, but John and George steadfastly refused. Finally, at a meeting with Allen Klein, John dropped his bombshell: "The group is over. I'm leaving." Since Klein was in the process of improving The Beatles' record deals, he asked John not to go public with his announcement until he had completed his negotiations. Reluctantly, John agreed.

Klein had discovered that The Beatles' contractual affairs were still far from clear. They had mistakenly believed that *Yellow Submarine* constituted the final film of their original three-film deal with United Artists—indeed, that had been the only reason they'd agreed to their minimal involvement with the project in the first place. Evidently they had been mistaken, and still owed United Artists one more movie. Klein saw an obvious solution: the "Get Back" project could be resuscitated and turned into a feature-length film.

The four Beatles continued to have very little to do with the "Get Back" project—now retitled "Let It Be" after one of Paul's songs on the album. With The Beatles' consent, Allen Klein handed the master tapes over to Phil Spector to see what he could come up with. The results were not uniformly appreciated. While John didn't much care what happened to them, Spector's elaborate doctoring of the album—in particular his use of lush orchestration—angered Paul McCartney, who publicly declared that he would have preferred the original versions to have been left on the album. In March 1970, Paul contacted John to tell him that he now intended to leave the group. With John having maintained his silence for six months, it was Paul McCartney who, on April 10, 1970, notified the world's press of his decision to quit The Beatles. The news was confirmed on the press release accompanying his own debut album, *McCartney*, which was issued seven days later. John was cynical about the timing of Paul's announcement, but admitted to feeling a grudging admiration for Paul's tactics: "I was a fool not to do it ... to use it to sell a record," he later carped.

The Beatles were now dead, though few were completely surprised by the time the official announcement came. The group had been immensely popular, both in critical and commercial terms. Each member was world-famous and inspired a great deal of public affection. It was therefore almost inevitable that the individual ex-Beatles would enjoy successful solo careers. Indeed, although John Lennon enjoyed immense success during the 1970s, his former partner (and rival) Paul McCartney would become arguably the most successful solo artist of the decade. Even if much of that success was due to his peddling what John disparagingly referred to as "grandma music."

The end of the Fabs: The Beatles during their final photoshoot together, August 1969.

Kicking over the traces

While The Beatles limped toward an inevitable breakup, John Lennon channeled his creative energy into The Plastic Ono Band. For their third single, John hired legendary producer Phil Spector, who was in London to discuss sorting out the "Get Back" tapes with Allen Klein, now officially acting as The Beatles' manager. The single "Instant Karma!" was the result of this fascinating collaboration. It was the closest John ever came to achieving the spontaneity he now sought in his music-making. He wrote the song one morning in late January 1970, and recorded it a few days later with Alan White, Klaus Voormann, George Harrison on lead guitar, and Billy Preston—who had played keyboards with The Beatles during the "Get Back" sessions—on electric piano. Within two weeks it was in the shops.

To promote the single John appeared on *Top Of The Pops*—the first Beatle to do so since 1966. His appearance came as a shock to many of his ardent fans: both he and Yoko had ushered in the new decade by cropping their long hair. They gave their locks to Black Power leader Michael X, in exchange for a pair of bloodstained boxing shorts once owned by Muhammad Ali. The Lennons later auctioned the shorts for a peace cause.

At the end of September 1970, John moved into Abbey Road with Phil Spector to record The Plastic Ono Band's first studio album. Featuring Ringo on drums, Klaus Voormann on bass, and Billy Preston on keyboards, the album took barely four weeks to complete and was issued two weeks before Christmas 1970. John's public was by now a little wary of the unpredictability of his new offerings. However the album, released as *John Lennon/Plastic Ono Band*, abandoned his experimental leanings in favor of a brutally stark and intense set of songs; Dr. Janov's therapy was a clear influence. Songs such as "Mother" and "My Mummy's Dead" drew on his childhood loss to produce a belated public mourning, while "Working Class Hero" was a sarcastic attack on the values instilled into him during that childhood. It is perhaps the album's central piece—"God"—that gives the clearest picture of Lennon's outlook on life at this time. The song is a dry-eyed rejection of everything from religion and mysticism to Elvis Presley and, ultimately, The Beatles. The dream was over.

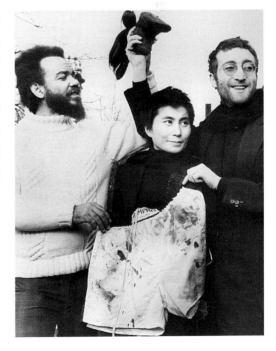

Opposite: John and a blindfolded Yoko on *Top Of The Pops*, 1970.
Right: On February 4, 1970, John and Yoko cut their hair and gave the shorn locks to Black Power leader Michael X in exchange for a pair of Muhammad Ali's boxing shorts. Both the hair and the shorts were later to be auctioned for peace and other good causes.

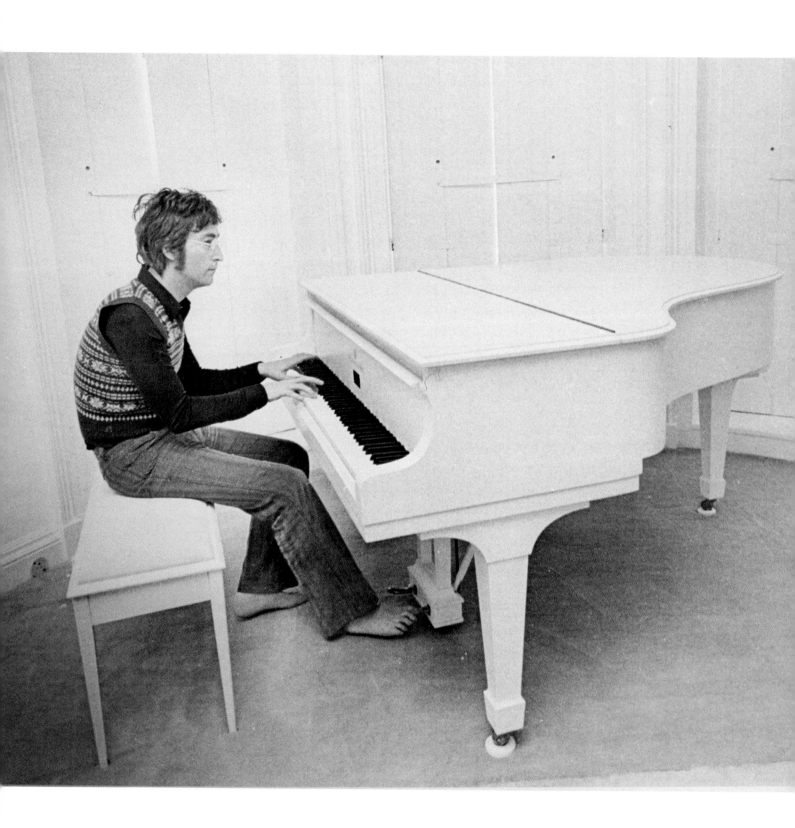

Imagine

John Lennon/Plastic Ono Band was a qualified commercial success, reaching number 11 in the U.K. albums chart. At this point in his life, its position mattered little to John–if the public still wanted to listen to his music, then it would have to be on his terms.

The year 1971 kicked off with a promotional trip to the States. While he was there, John upped his growing credibility with the political "underground" by mixing with controversial radicals such as Jerry Rubin and Abbie Hoffman, often raising money for their causes. If any further proof of his growing politicization were needed, it came in the form of the single "Power To The People," which was no less than a call for mass proletarian action. In the eyes of the U.S. authorities, John was now seen as an "undesirable," a situation that would create numerous practical difficulties for the Lennons over the years that followed. As a footnote, John would later disown the track, claiming that it was a "guilt song" written to appease radical figures who were skeptical of a multimillionaire celebrity with such views.

In July of 1971, John turned his home Tittenhurst Park into a makeshift recording studio where, once again under the guidance of Phil Spector, a new album was recorded. This time the sound was somewhat mellow–lavish, even–and the harsh, cynical lyrics that made its predecessor so hard-hitting were toned down. Credited simply to "John Lennon," it would turn out to be his most famous album: indeed, the title track would be one of the most popular songs ever written–"Imagine."

The inspiration for "Imagine" came, unsurprisingly, from Yoko Ono. In 1964 she published a book of poetry called *Grapefruit* (republished in 1971) in which each piece asked the reader to "imagine" a given scenario. John later admitted that he should have given Yoko a co-writing credit for the song that would eventually become his most famous solo composition, but "I was still full of wanting my own space after being in a room with the guys all the time, having to share things."

Many people have commented on the irony of a fabulously wealthy young man sitting in his mansion, asking the rest of the world to "Imagine no possessions ...," but John repeatedly claimed that the song was a sincere statement. And whatever the personal circumstances of the songwriter himself, the song's simple beauty undeniably still hits home.

In spite of its melodic tunefulness and lush strings, John nevertheless saw the album as coming from the same source as its more "difficult" predecessor: "The first record was too real for people, so nobody bought it ... " he reasoned. "You see, *Imagine* was exactly the same message, just sugar-coated ... Now I understand what you have to do. Put your political point across with a little honey."

John recorded probably his best-loved album, *Imagine*, at his Tittenhurst Park home in 1971.

John versus Paul

With *Imagine*, John Lennon became the potent commercial force that most people expected an ex-Beatle to be. Both the album and the single of the same name became massive global hits. But although The Beatles were now dead and buried as far as John was concerned, his relationship with Paul McCartney was becoming increasingly fractious and public.

Even back in the days of The Quarrymen there had been rivalry between John and Paul. Paul's superior musical skills represented a threat to John's unequivocal authority. Throughout the haze of Beatlemania, Paul had always resented John's perceived role as the band's unofficial leader, and the way John's extracurricular activities resulted in him being dubbed the "intellectual Beatle" by the media. Paul didn't much care for the influence Yoko Ono had over John's work either. For his part, John came to resent the way Paul thrust himself into the driving seat following the death of Brian Epstein.

By the time of *The White Album*, the two were also pursuing different musical aims. John was keen to mine the depths of his soul for inspiration and catharsis, irrespective of whether his public wanted to hear it. Paul seemed happy to continue being one of the greatest pop songwriters of the century and a gifted multi-instrumentalist. The bust-up over The Beatles' management was the first sign of bitterness between Lennon and McCartney. The timing of Paul's debut LP and the announcement of his decision to leave The Beatles—even though he'd known that John had effectively left six months earlier—clearly rankled with Lennon. A public squabble was born between the two that soon found its way into their music.

Paul's solo career got off to a flying start. He wrote and played virtually every note of his 1970 debut album, *McCartney*; it had been a big seller and a critical success. However, his 1971 follow-up, *Ram*, included a number of lyrics that John saw as jibes at himself and Yoko, notably the song "Too Many People (Going Underground)." John's stinging response was the bitterest track on the *Imagine* album. "How Do You Sleep?" was an extraordinary personal attack in which John cast the ultimate insult: "The sound you make is Muzak to my ears." As a final, childish gesture, the album featured a photograph of John grappling with a pig—a parody of the cover of *Ram* showing a rustic Paul posing with a sheep on his Scottish farm.

The sparring spilled over into the music press, when Paul made some derogatory remarks about his ex-partner in a *Melody Maker* interview. Two weeks later, John contacted the paper's editor, requesting that his vitriolic response be printed in full.

The wounds created by the encounters ran very deep. It would be four years before the two men came face to face again, and thereafter they enjoyed only periodic contact.

Like John and Yoko, Paul and Linda McCartney (seen here in 1970) made music together. Both pairings attracted critical flak, though Paul's group Wings was hugely successful in the 1970s.

5 The Final Years

In 1971, John and Yoko set up home in New York City, where
they mix with artists, intellectuals, and political revolutionaries.
John's music changes, but a new hard edge alienates many
of his former fans. A turbulent period sees him estranged from
Yoko, but after they are reunited, he retires into domesticity,
concentrating on raising their newborn son. Returning from
a recording session on December 8, 1980, John Lennon is
shot dead outside his home. The life of one of the most
extraordinary artists of the twentieth century is over.

War is over!

After the breakup of The Beatles, John and Yoko spent more and more time in New York City, ostensibly fighting for custody of Yoko's daughter, Kyoko Cox. Early in 1971, the duo decided to live in the U.S. permanently. John welcomed the move:

"It's Yoko's old stamping ground, and she felt the country would be more receptive to what we're up to ... in the United States we're treated like artists. Which we are! But here I'm like the lad who knew Paul, got a lucky break, won the pools, and married the actress."

"In New York there's these 20 or 30 artists who all understand what I'm doing and have the same kind of mind as me. It's just like heaven after being here ... you've seen how they treat me in the press."

On September 3, 1971, John and Yoko caught a flight to New York from London's Heathrow Airport. Unknown to John, he would never set foot on English soil again.

John and Yoko's first New York recording session took place little more than a month later. They called on Phil Spector's production skills for what has since become a Christmas classic—"Happy Xmas (War Is Over)." The chorus, sung by John, Yoko, and children from the Harlem Baptist Choir, first appeared as part of their peace protests in 1969—in 11 major cities across the world, the couple hired billboards to display their own personal Christmas card: "WAR IS OVER! IF YOU WANT IT. Happy Christmas from John & Yoko."

After the success of *Imagine*, John's first U.S. album came as a major disappointment. A return to the spontaneity of his early efforts, *Some Time In New York City* was completed in just 19 days. And it showed. Much of the album contained trite political sloganeering, taking on a cross section of the popular issues of the day: sexual inequality ("Woman Is The Nigger Of The World"); Northern Ireland ("Sunday Bloody Sunday" and "The Luck Of The Irish"); and jailed political activists ("Angela," "John Sinclair," and "Attica State"). They may have been sincere statements, but they were not eloquently made. Packaged with the almost unlistenable *Live Jam* free album, *Some Time In New York City* barely made the Top 50 in the U.S. The criticisms that his lyrics had become simplistic and that he was just churning out received opinions from the intellectuals in his circle were hard for Lennon to swallow.

He later acknowledged that the album nearly wrecked his career. Although the U.S. would forgive and forget when it came to each new Lennon release, his popularity in the U.K. dived.

In December 1969, John and Yoko had paid for their slogan "WAR IS OVER! IF YOU WANT IT" to be displayed on 2,000 billboards in 11 cities worldwide in time for Christmas.

Public enemy

John Lennon loved New York City and the seemingly boundless opportunities that the United States offered. Indeed, he went as far as making his thoughts on the matter very public. "I profoundly regret that I was not born an American," he announced shortly after his arrival, doubtless further alienating members of his U.K. fan-base in the process. Lennon disliked the petty-minded way in which the U.K. press treated Yoko and himself. Moreover, as a couple of tracks on *Some Time In New York City* indicated, he was angry at the British government's attitude to the "Troubles" in Northern Ireland. However, dark forces had been at work in an effort to keep him out of the U.S. ever since he and Yoko had first visited the country.

John's open association with radical Marxists, Black Panthers, and other revolutionary groups had created powerful enemies, most notably President Nixon and FBI chief, J. Edgar Hoover. His phones were tapped and he became aware that intelligence officers were shadowing his private life, constantly digging for "dirt" that could be used as evidence against him. Because John had a 1968 drug conviction on his records, obtaining a visa to remain in the U.S. was always going to be difficult for him. At the end of February 1972, his temporary visa ran out and he was informed that a new one would not be issued. He was given two months to leave the United States.

The root of the problem lay in a report from a Senate subcommittee dealing with internal security, which claimed that in 1968 John Lennon had bankrolled a "revolutionary" group that had sabotaged the 1968 Democratic Convention. He was now thought to be financing a plot to have President Nixon ousted at the 1972 Republican Convention. Although John denied the charges, it was clear the U.S. government viewed him as a highly unwelcome guest. At the time, the FBI suggested that a narcotics charge would be the easiest grounds on which to have Lennon deported. Why this threat was never carried out is something of a mystery, as it was the one area in which John Lennon was clearly in violation of U.S. law.

His lawyers fought a fierce campaign to have his visa renewed. However, John's trump card was an appearance on the nationally televised Dick Cavett chat show, in which he described the extent of the government's harassment to a sympathetic U.S. public.

There were frequent legal battles over the next four years, and it was not until July 27, 1976, that John Lennon was awarded the coveted Green Card, allowing him unlimited stay in the United States. Prior to that date he had been too scared to leave the country in case he was not allowed back in. But even after securing permanent residency, he still never found the will to return to England.

Dark days: John arrives at the offices of the Immigration and Naturalization Service on May 12, 1972, to fight moves for his deportation.

Beatles to get back?

The success of The Beatles cast a long shadow over each of the members' solo careers. In public, John, Paul, George, and Ringo usually only discussed The Beatles when journalists asked that one burning question—would the Fab Four ever get together again?

It's clear that none of the ex-Beatles would have gained much from a reunion, short of bolstering their already swollen bank accounts. And in any case, by 1973, all four were successful solo performers. John Lennon and Paul McCartney were chart regulars, while George Harrison had scored a handful of hits, among them "My Sweet Lord," the biggest-selling single of 1971. Even Ringo, who as the drummer might have been expected to fall by the wayside, enjoyed a splendidly eccentric pop career of his own in the early 1970s.

The talk of reunions was often fueled by occasions that featured various permutations of the band. The first came in 1971 when George Harrison and Ravi Shankar organized a benefit concert for UNICEF, the charity that at the time was struggling to bring aid to starving children in Bangladesh. The aim was to raise $25,000. George arranged for some of rock's top stars to perform for no fee and, as a matter of course, the other three ex-Beatles were all invited. At first it looked as though they might play—albeit not as "The Beatles." However, the speculation about it in the music press proved too much for Paul McCartney, who pulled out. Then, when it became clear that Yoko had not been invited, John also withdrew.

Ringo Starr's 1973 album *Ringo* was the closest the four Beatles ever came to recording together (at least until the posthumous recording of John's "Free As A Bird" in 1994). But while each Beatle made an appearance on the LP, no single track featured them all.

Toward the end of the 1970s there were several attempts to revive The Beatles. One was initiated by Paul McCartney—by then the only ex-Beatle still having regular hits. In 1979, proposing a concert for the benefit of Kampuchean refugees, Paul said he would be prepared to share the stage with his three former colleagues. George and Ringo agreed to the idea, but John wanted nothing to do with it. Although their personal differences were now long in the past, John dismissed the idea with the line "we'd just be four rusty old men."

In September of the same year, promoter Sid Bernstein made a public appeal to The Beatles in the pages of the *New York Times*. He wanted to put on a series of benefit concerts for the Vietnamese Boat People, which he believed could raise up to $500 million—The Beatles were to be his star attraction. Two weeks later Kurt Waldheim, then General Secretary of the United Nations, joined in the plea. It was all to no avail. Only John's murder on December 8, 1980, put a permanent end to speculation about a Beatles reunion.

Ringo and George (left and center) teamed up for the charity Bangladesh concert in 1971. A number of other stars appeared, including Bob Dylan (right).

Mind Games

When John and Yoko arrived in New York City, they first headed for the hip artistic atmosphere of Greenwich Village. However, by 1973 John was tiring of his image as a radical and becoming disillusioned with figures such as Jerry Rubin and Abbie Hoffman who, he felt, were "all talk." In March 1973, he and Yoko abandoned the easygoing Village in favor of the celebrity stylings of the Dakota Building, a luxury apartment overlooking Central Park.

For the first time in their five-year relationship, the Lennons were no longer an inseparable couple. Still smarting from the failure of *Some Time In New York City*, John frittered his time away while Yoko pursued her own artistic career. The rumors doing the rounds were that rock's most famous couple were not getting on too well.

John's record contract dictated that he must have a new album ready for release each year. But in 1973 he was feeling no great desire to go into the studio. During the sessions for his new album he confessed to an interviewer: "It's getting to be work. It's ruining the music ... Every time I strap on a guitar it's the same old jazz." And it's a mood that comes through on much of the resulting album.

Released in November 1973, *Mind Games* came as relief to most Lennon fans, as it signaled a return to the lush melodicism of *Imagine*. Gone were the political rantings of its predecessor that some had found a little embarrassing. Gone, too, were the rough-edged performances of old—John had opted to surround himself with some of New York's top session men. (Ironically, the lead guitarist on *Mind Games*, David Spinozza, had also played on Paul McCartney's *Ram*, the album that prompted John to pen the vitriolic "How Do You Sleep?") But although *Mind Games* contained gems such as the title track and the gentle ballad "I Know (I Know)," the overall feeling was that John Lennon was treading water. John himself seemed to agree as he defensively justified the LP's existence: "It's just an album ... there's no very deep message about it. The only reason I make albums is because you're supposed to." The problems in the Lennons' relationship were subtly mirrored in the album's sleeve. The front cover shows Yoko's face in profile, forming a mountainlike background, in front of which is a photograph of John. On the back cover, the image of John is much larger. May Pang, the Lennons' personal assistant, later alleged that John saw this as a metaphor for him walking away from Yoko.

For all its flaws, *Mind Games* went some way to repairing the commercial damage of *Some Time In New York City*. The album and "Mind Games" the single became minor hits on both sides of the Atlantic.

John and Yoko were experts at generating publicity and frequently held press conferences to promote their latest artistic endeavor or to draw attention to a deserving cause.

Leaving Yoko

Mind Games had emerged in the midst of a creative lull. As someone who required constant stimulation, this period made John difficult to live with, especially as Yoko continued to progress with her own work. Moreover, his endless mood swings were made worse by heavy drinking bouts. Realizing their relationship was going nowhere, Yoko told her husband that she felt a temporary separation was necessary. As John would later comment: "She don't [sic] suffer fools gladly, even if she's married to him."

Initially, John was not keen on Yoko's decision: "She kicked me out, pure and simple," he commented, bitterly. Later, he came to respect it, grudgingly admitting: "It was grow up time and I'm glad she made me do it."

Yoko suggested that John move to Los Angeles. There was no question of him leaving the country, due to his continuing Green Card problems, and Yoko felt that John should experience the City of Angels and the Californian lifestyle. She also made the bold suggestion that he take their secretary May Pang to look after him. Born in New York of Chinese parents, 22-year-old May Pang had worked as secretary to the Lennons' company Lennono for several years, and was a trusted employee. Yoko understood that John would be helpless alone in California. Although he could drive, he was invariably chauffeured around wherever he wanted to go. He'd never had to engage in normal activities such as going to supermarkets or paying bills—someone else had always done it for him.

In October 1973, John and May Pang arrived in Los Angeles for what would in many ways turn into a 15-month rampage that saw John transform himself into an appallingly clichéd rock-and-roll animal. In something of an understatement, he would later say of this period, "the feminist side of me died slightly."

Even though John and Yoko would still speak on the phone up to 20 times a day, he quickly formed an intimate relationship with May Pang. She would later write a controversial account of their affair, entitled *John Lennon: The Lost Weekend*. The intimacy that Pang describes developing between the two of them was disputed by Elliot Mintz, John's closest friend in America and one of the few people he knew when he arrived in Los Angeles. Mintz claimed: "To think that John ran off with May to leave Yoko Ono would require a remarkable suspension of logic." As far as he was concerned, "It was not a love affair. It was a relationship born out of the convenience of the moment." However, Mintz did believe that Yoko all but sanctioned the affair: "I suppose Yoko knew it was likely there would be intimacy between them. She took a mature view knowing John: 'Better with May than galloping around with the golden groupies.'"

May and John at the premiere of the musical *Sgt. Pepper's Lonely Hearts Club Band*, November 1974.

The Lost Weekend

John's separation from Yoko resulted in his life spiraling out of control. John later said he felt "like an elephant in a zoo." Whatever the cause, the period that became known as "The Lost Weekend" saw John going well and truly off the rails. Yoko may have hoped that California would help to invigorate John's creative appetite, but on arrival in LA he teamed up with some of rock's most notorious wastrels—Ringo Starr, Keith Moon (drummer with The Who), and singer Harry Nilsson among others—and embarked on one long alcoholic binge.

In fact, the madness may well have been less over the top than posterity records. The problem for Lennon and his Rat Pack was that their scenes of debauchery always took place in public, and so were always reported by the media. According to John, his drug intake had been so vast during the final days of The Beatles that he was left with a low body resistance to alcohol. As his friend Elliot Mintz recalled, he was such a poor drinker that "if he had one glass of wine I'd have to cancel all appointments for the next three days." The booze also made him boorish and argumentative: "He would start an argument and keep it going just for the sake of having a row and winning it," Mintz remembered.

One one occasion, returning from a vodka binge to the house in Bel Air that record producer Lou Adler had loaned him and May, John began to smash the place up. He launched vases at stained-glass windows and trashed the gold discs that hung on the wall. Phil Spector and his bodyguard were present, and wrestled the out-of-control Lennon to his bed, where they bound his hands and feet to stop him from doing any more damage to the house or to himself. John's personal nadir came in March 1974 at the Troubadour Club in Los Angeles during a show by The Smothers Brothers, featuring his old friend Tommy Smothers. Drunk on arrival, his constant foul-mouthed heckling ruined the evening for the rest of the audience. When Ken Fritz, manager of The Smothers Brothers, tried to shut Lennon up he was assaulted. Lennon ended the evening by slapping waitress Brenda Mary Perkins, who tried to take a photograph of the fiasco. Her claim for damages against Lennon was later dismissed in court, but Perkins was sanguine about the experience: "It's not the pain that hurts," she explained, "it's finding out that one of your idols is a real asshole."

Throughout the turmoil John continued his regular telephone dialog with Yoko. According to Mintz: "All of his thoughts, all of his longings had to do with his desperation to get back with Yoko, and to his frustration with her telling him he didn't sound ready." Little did John know that, in spite of his present erratic behavior, Yoko always believed their reunion was simply a matter of time.

Even during his "lost" year with May Pang (in background), John kept in touch with his son Julian (left). However, he always felt guilty that he had not taken a more active role in Julian's upbringing.

Rock-and-roll fiasco

John's arrival in California had coincided with the release of *Mind Games*. Although aware that the album had been a half-hearted effort, he was nevertheless disappointed at the mauling it received at the hands of the world's music press. He felt further dispirited when he realized that Ringo Starr's surprise hit album *Ringo* was outpacing his new offering by some distance. The final ignominy came in 1974 when Paul McCartney's band Wings hit peak form with *Band On The Run*, an album that sold in Beatlesque proportions.

Although he often portrayed himself as tough and impenetrable, at heart John Lennon was a ball of insecurity. He now began to feel that his life—both private and artistic—was falling apart. He needed something to focus on, a project he could become fired up about.

Eventually, he turned to an idea that he'd had in mind for some time, and decided he would record an album of old rock-and-roll classics. His working title was "Oldies But Mouldies"—a parody of a 1966 Beatles hits compilation, *A Collection Of Beatles Oldies ... But Goldies*. As a songwriter, his confidence had reached rock bottom; such a project would take the pressure off having to come up with new material. Furthermore, with a charismatic producer such as Phil Spector at the helm, John wouldn't be forced to make too many artistic decisions of his own.

There was one other benefit to this project. Several years earlier, music publisher Morris Levy threatened to sue John for plagiarism. Levy owned the publishing rights to most of Chuck Berry's classic rock-and-roll hits and claimed that on "Come Together" from *Abbey Road*, John had borrowed heavily from Berry's 1956 hit "You Can't Catch Me." Although the claim was tenuous, John couldn't face more litigation and so agreed out of court to record a number of other Levy-owned Chuck Berry songs for a future album.

The sessions for the album quickly turned into a drunken fiasco. Spector's behavior grew stranger by the day—increasingly paranoid, he would sometimes pull out a revolver and pump the occasional bullet into the studio walls. In spite of an all-star cast that included Dr. John, ace session musician Leon Russell, and members of The Rolling Stones, almost $100,000 was spent on recording and only four of the many tracks laid down were considered usable. Finally, the working relationship between John Lennon and his producer broke down completely, and Spector disappeared, taking the master tapes with him. He returned to his heavily guarded mansion and Lennon was initially unable to get him to surrender the tapes. Even when Spector obliged, Lennon realized they were of dubious quality to say the least. Both his personal and professional lives now seemed to be in stalemate.

Although both men had been called musical geniuses, John's collaboration with Phil Spector on his album of rock-and-roll classics proved to be a disastrous experience for all concerned.

Walls And Bridges

With his album of rock-and-roll covers on hold, and the worst of his LA excesses behind him, John began work on an album of new material. But even though he now lived on the opposite coast to his wife, Yoko Ono remained the principle inspiration for *Walls And Bridges*. Indeed, many of the songs can be easily interpreted as a direct plea for Yoko to take him back and get him out of the mess he now found himself in. Even the album's title may have alluded to the barriers that now separated John from his soul mate, despite the fact that John facetiously claimed it had actually been "sent from above in the guise of a public service announcement."

Walls And Bridges spawned two major hit singles: "#9 Dream," appropriately enough, reached number 9 on the U.S. charts, while the irreverent "Whatever Gets You Thru The Night," featuring Elton John on keyboards and backing vocals, gave Lennon his first solo chart-topping single in the States. However, the album's key moment is the closing ballad "Nobody Loves You (When You're Down And Out)"—the title is a play on that of an old blues song by Jimmie Cox. A cynical (some might say self-pitying) assessment of the state of his world by the middle of 1974, John himself admitted it "exactly expressed the period I was apart from Yoko." Elsewhere on the album, his lyrics were equally revealing. "Scared"—which could almost be "Help!" 10 years on—has its author admitting "I'm so tired of being alone."

In a reflection of its autobiographical nature, *Walls And Bridges* came complete with a lavish sleeve, including a booklet featuring the lyrics and illustrated by drawings and paintings that John had made when he was 12 years old.

Although it gave John his biggest hit since *Imagine*, and restored his public profile, he was never hugely taken with *Walls And Bridges*:

"This last year has been an extraordinary one for me personally. And I'm almost amazed that I could get *anything* out. Musically my mind was a clutter. [*Walls And Bridges*] was the work of a semi-sick craftsman. There was no inspiration and it gave an aura of misery."

John's dismissal of the album is not surprising given that it must have represented a powerful document of a period in which his personal life had reached rock bottom. In truth, *Walls And Bridges* may not have been vintage Lennon, but it was nonetheless a fine record. May Pang has challenged the accepted view that John's life during this period had been one year-long "lost weekend," arguing that he produced some of the best music of his solo career. *Walls And Bridges* does much to back up her claim.

John pictured during a photosession for the cover of the album *Walls And Bridges,* in 1974.

New inspiration

Hanging out with other musicians in LA had not been overly healthy or productive for John Lennon. His early cohorts in drunken mayhem had been Harry Nilsson and Keith Moon—neither being particularly known for their high productivity (nor, for that matter, their sanity). But by the time of the *Walls And Bridge*s sessions, Lennon was beginning to get back on track. A key player in this turnaround was Elton John, at that time emerging as the most successful British artist in the U.S. since the heyday of The Beatles. An extremely hard-working and commercially astute musician, Elton provided Lennon with some badly needed stimulation and direction.

The collaboration began when Lennon played Elton a demo tape of the songs that would make up *Walls And Bridges*, and asked him to contribute some piano and backing vocals to a track of his choice. Like many pop stars of the time, The Beatles had been an important inspiration for Elton during his teenage years, and even though he was now a massive star in his own right, he was more than happy to oblige. The number he chose was "Whatever Gets You Thru The Night"—not necessarily the best song in the collection (Lennon himself regarded it as his least favorite), but Elton felt it was easily the most commercial. However, there was a price to pay: if it topped the chart, Elton demanded that Lennon repay the favor by performing at one of his forthcoming shows.

Amazingly, on November 16, 1974, "Whatever Gets You Thru The Night" arrived at the top of the U.S. singles chart, and Elton called in his debt. Two weeks later, at Elton's Thanksgiving Day show at New York's Madison Square Garden, John Lennon appeared on stage as a surprise guest star in front of an ecstatic audience, and performed three songs with the show's star. In addition to his chart-topping single, they duetted on a version of John's "Lucy In The Sky With Diamonds." The brief set ended with "I Saw Her Standing There," a song from The Beatles' first album. As if to signal a gradual mellowing of his spiky character, Lennon poignantly dedicated it "to an old estranged fiancé of mine, called Paul." It would be the last time John Lennon appeared on a public stage.

After the show, Elton's record label threw a party at New York's plush Pierre Hotel. Although Lennon wasn't aware of it at the time, Yoko had been in the audience that night and she was also one of the guests at the aftershow bash; her appearance both shocked and delighted him. That evening marked the start of their reconciliation.

Opposite: The two Johns—Elton and Lennon, Madison Square Garden, 1974.
Right: The concert was to be Lennon's last public performance.

Rock and roller

The year 1974 ended in a whirlwind of activity. With publisher Morris Levy breathing down his neck, chasing the fulfillment of their out-of-court agreement, Lennon had deliberately ended *Walls And Bridges* with a vignette of Lee Dorsey's "Ya Ya"–another song owned by Levy. He had hoped this gesture would be enough to get Levy off his back. He was wrong. Levy demanded that Lennon cover at least three numbers from his catalog.

In an effort to settle the matter once and for all, John retrieved the "Oldies But Mouldies" master tapes from Phil Spector. However, after listening to them again he told May Pang that they were "awful ... I must have felt terrible when I did these." Only three tracks were usable– even for an album driven by contractual fulfillments, John still had certain standards to maintain. At the end of October, in four highly charged days at the Record Plant studios, he recorded and mixed 10 more rock-and-roll classics. The resulting album–now renamed *Rock 'n' Roll*–was less a faithful recreation of the spirit of the 1950s than a nostalgic revisiting of the soundtrack of John's youth. The overall effect was affectionate rather than rip-roaring, but each track has the imprint of John's personality firmly stamped on it.

All things considered, John made the best job of a bad situation. Released in February 1975, only four months after *Walls And Bridges*, *Rock 'n' Roll* was another sizable success, with the single "Stand By Me" becoming a U.S. Top 10 chart hit. In a way, by turning his back on contemporary music for basic rock and roll, John was even mirroring the punk explosion that would soon hit the world.

One of the most attractive aspects of the album was the photograph chosen for the sleeve. Taken by The Beatles' German friend Jürgen Vollmer in Hamburg in 1961, it shows John as a sneering 21-year-old Teddy Boy leaning against the stage door to a club.

Closing the album with Lloyd Price's "Just Because," John parodied one of the clichés of rock-and-roll balladry with a talkover sequence. In the manner of the last song of the evening, as the ending fades away he offers the listener a fond "goodnight." But even as he was recording the song, he found himself wondering "Am I really saying farewell to the music business? I looked at the cover I'd chosen ... I thought, this is some sort of cosmic thing. Here I am with this old picture of me in Hamburg in '61 and I'm saying farewell from the Record Plant, and I'm ending as I started, singing this straight rock 'n' roll stuff."

Having resuscitated his flagging career, John Lennon was now once more a commercial force in the music world. It therefore seems ironic in retrospect that it would be another five years before he set foot in a recording studio again.

John chose a moody photograph of himself taken in Hamburg in 1961 for the cover of the *Rock 'n' Roll* album. He later reflected that he felt he had come full circle with the record.

A big month

October 1975 turned out to be an important month for the Lennons. The ball started rolling on October 8, when John received news about his legal battle to stay in America. The signs were good: New York State's Supreme Court had voted by a two-to-one decision to reverse his latest deportation order. The residing judge was unequivocal in his judgment, stating: "The court cannot condone selective deportation based upon secret political grounds."

America's prevailing political wind was in the throes of change. Two years earlier, former president Richard Nixon had resigned in disgrace under the cloud of Watergate. His successor, Gerald Ford, had finally taken the U.S. military out of Vietnam. Furthermore, a new Democrat administration under Jimmy Carter was preparing itself for office. By the mid-1970s John Lennon was no longer viewed as a subversive—indeed, the authorities were sympathetic to his cause. The court decision enabled John to finally obtain a Green Card in 1976. He was told that after five years he could apply for full U.S. citizenship.

At 2 a.m. on October 9, Yoko Ono gave birth to a son, Sean Taro Ono Lennon. The date also marked John's 35th birthday, and he was ecstatic: "I feel higher than the Empire State Building," he announced, joyously. The first person he called with the news was Aunt Mimi.

John had always been acutely aware of the legacy that his own parental instability had left him. Consequently, he had already tried, with some success, to establish a meaningful relationship with his first son, Julian, who by this time was in his early teens. But John was adamant Sean wouldn't have to face the same hardships that he'd been through himself.

Four months after Sean entered his life, John Lennon's recording contract with EMI/Capitol expired. Heralding his new intentions, he decided not to bother renewing it. For the next four years, John had virtually no involvement in the music world. With Yoko employed in looking after the Lennons' business affairs, John became a self-styled house-husband, channeling all of his energy into Sean's upbringing. While Yoko worked, John and Sean were rarely apart. John took care of the washing, cleaning, and changing diapers—his new domesticity even stretched as far as cookery. This was clearly not the same person who had been screaming for world revolution less than five years earlier.

John's antipathy to the music business also extended to old friends. He was especially contemptuous of the music Paul McCartney and Mick Jagger were making in the mid-1970s. He saw no development in their work and dismissed them collectively as the "Rolling Wings." In a waspish put-down, he also compared Paul to middle-of-the-road balladeer Engelbert Humperdinck. The music-making part of John's life was over. For now.

Beautiful boy. After his son Sean was born in 1975, John dedicated himself to bringing him up. To do so he turned his back on the music business and was not to release another album for five years.

Domestic bliss

Placing his financial affairs in the hands of an avant-garde artist might have seemed like a risk for John, but it turned out to be a wise move. Yoko Ono quickly revealed that she had a phenomenally good head for business affairs, even if her intuitive methods—she was especially fond of using numerology and tarot readings for guidance—were hardly orthodox. Yoko invested in property, agriculture, works of art, and many ecologically sound projects. By the end of the decade, under her guiding hand, Lennono—their joint company—was conservatively valued at $150 million.

Meanwhile, John had turned into something approaching a health freak. He baked his own bread, followed macrobiotic regimes, paid scrupulous attention to his and Sean's diets, and banned alcohol from the Dakota Building. However, he never managed to end his lifelong love of caffeine and cigarettes.

In 1977, secure in the knowledge that they could now safely leave America and be allowed to return, the Lennons embarked on a two-month trip to Japan. John loved the country. He was particularly fascinated by the rituals of a culture that was so alien to him. Moreover, he appreciated the fact that he could walk the streets of Tokyo and remain largely unrecognized. The outside world hardly got a look in during this period in the ex-Beatle's life. John paid little attention to contemporary music, and the changing climate of punk and new wave that was then transforming the world of rock and roll largely passed him by. He and Yoko were enjoying a period of long-overdue domestic contentment.

However, wherever he was in the world, John would invariably phone Aunt Mimi on most days. In July 1980, he gave her a glimpse of his future intentions: "I'm 40 this year. I'm going to make one more record, Mimi, then I'm going to do some writing," he confided.

John had made his decision in July when he was on holiday in Bermuda. He rented a house for a month, during which time he was planning to relax, swim, and sail. However, as it turned out, within a week he was writing songs. Back in New York, John and Yoko spent much of August and September in the studio. But these sessions were like no previous recordings in which John Lennon had been involved—they were civilized affairs, free from alcohol and drugs, both of which were now strictly forbidden. The music that resulted reflected both the relaxed atmosphere in which it was recorded, and John and Yoko's contentment with each other.

During his stay in Bermuda, John visited the Botanical Gardens and came across a freesia that bore a name he instinctively seized upon for the title of the new album. It seemed to perfectly reflect his life with Yoko: "Double Fantasy."

After Sean reached the age of five, John and Yoko began to appear in public more frequently.

End of an era

Fast approaching 40, and with his son Sean now of nursery age, John Lennon rediscovered his thirst to make music: "I swore I'd look after that boy until he was five ... " he revealed in one interview. "He's five now and I feel like getting back to my music. The urge is there. It's been a long time since I wrote a song, but they're coming thick and fast now."

The reports that John was once again in the recording studio caused ripples of excitement in the music media. Unsurprisingly, there was no shortage of music corporations prepared to talk about a new record deal, although the all-out bidding war that might have been anticipated was tempered when the Lennons announced that the new release would be a "John and Yoko" album. Wary at the prospect of uncommercial Yoko offerings, some labels asked to hear demo tapes before committing themselves. John took this as an insult, and eventually signed a deal with the newly created Geffen Records; label boss David Geffen offered the Lennons a deal unconditionally, without hearing any of the new material.

October 27, 1980, saw the much-heralded release of the first new John Lennon single in five years. But "(Just Like) Starting Over" turned out to be an anticlimax for some people. Many had unrealistically high hopes for the return of one of the most important artists of the previous two decades. Even so, on the evidence of this piece of nostalgic whimsy it seemed unlikely the album would break new ground. However, the world welcomed John's return, and within weeks the single had eased itself into the Top 10 of most countries.

Three weeks later, *Double Fantasy* hit the shops, to a largely lukewarm critical response. For many fans of his solo work, John was at his best when he was venting his anger and frustration. The Lennon on display here was a contented man, at one with himself, and happy to tell the world that all that really mattered to him now was his family. Such domestic contentment didn't necessarily make for the most exhilarating music.

Nevertheless, by the start of December 1980, with both the single and album in the upper reaches of the charts, confidence was running high. Work was already progressing on a follow-up and John talked openly about undertaking a world tour in 1981, including a series of dates in Britain. Tragically, none of his plans would come to fruition.

Late on the night of December 8, 1980, returning from a recording session, John and Yoko were about to enter the Dakota Building when a voice called out "Mr. Lennon?" As John turned round in response, five bullets from a .38 revolver tore into his arm and back. Despite his wounds, he managed to stagger up six steps to the office of Jay Hastings, the Dakota desk clerk, where he collapsed, moaning "I'm shot."

Even toward the end of his life John made time for fans' requests for autographs. Occasionally, he and Yoko would even take on the fans who hung around the Dakota as hired help.

News hits the streets

Scenes of trauma and chaos followed the shooting. Yoko screamed for an ambulance; after covering John with his jacket, Jay Hastings pressed an alarm button that connected the Dakota Building directly with a local police precinct. Some two minutes later, a squad car arrived at the Dakota. There was no time to wait for medical assistance, and John was bundled into the car, which immediately sped off in the direction of the Roosevelt Hospital. Doctors massaged his heart in an effort to get it working again, but it was too late—he had already bled to death. After returning from the hospital, Yoko announced her husband's death to the world, along with a simple plea: "John loved and prayed for the human race. Please do the same for him."

The news of John's murder spread quickly over the world's airwaves. Many bulletins drew attention to the irony that the man who was arguably one of the most famous public preachers for peace since Gandhi and Dr. Martin Luther King, Jr. had, like them, died a sudden and violent death.

On December 10, 1980, John Lennon was cremated at Hartsdale Crematorium, in New York State. He was mourned by millions across the world. On December 14, Yoko requested that his fans observe a worldwide 10-minute silence. Nearly half a million people gathered in New York's Central Park, opposite the Dakota, to pay their respects.

What of his assassin? Mark David Chapman was a 25-year-old former hospital security guard who had arrived in New York several days earlier. A Beatles fanatic, he had stayed at the Olcott Hotel on West 72nd Street—a short walk from John's home. On the day of the murder he had waited outside the Dakota with his copy of *Double Fantasy*, which he managed to get John to autograph for him. Arrested at the scene of his crime, the next day Mark Chapman was charged with murder and sentenced to life imprisonment.

Why would a devoted fan kill his hero? Repeated psychological examinations of Chapman failed to find a satisfactory answer. There were no signs that he was insane, even though he later claimed that God had visited him in his cell and told him to change his plea from not guilty to guilty (in doing so he avoided a trial). Chapman had clearly come to New York City with just one aim—to kill John Lennon.

Lennon's death generated a host of conspiracy theories. One, published by U.K. barrister Fenton Bresler, claimed there was evidence linking Chapman to the CIA. Given John's difficulties with the U.S. authorities, that wouldn't have been impossible. But now most people accept that Mark Chapman was solely responsible for John Lennon's violent murder.

Lennon signs a copy of *Double Fantasy* for Mark David Chapman outside the Dakota on December 8, 1980. Just a few hours later, Chapman shot Lennon dead.

The aftermath

During the media hysteria that surrounded John's death, sales of his music went into overdrive. Indeed, in a sad and ironic twist, the three months that followed saw his greatest period of commercial success as a solo artist. "(Just Like) Starting Over," which had slipped down the U.K. charts to number 21 from its original number 8 peak, did an about-face and leaped to number 1. When it vacated the top spot just before Christmas, 1980, it was replaced by the hastily reissued "Imagine." One position behind that sat "Happy Xmas (War Is Over)." In the new year, "Woman," a track that John himself had thought of as being particularly Beatlesque, provided the third posthumous Lennon U.K. number 1 in three months. "(Just Like) Starting Over" also hit the top spot in the States, while *Double Fantasy* became a transatlantic chart-topper.

Not surprisingly, the period following John's death was extremely painful for Yoko Ono. Radio stations paid tribute to her husband by playing his music endlessly. There was no escaping his legacy—for weeks to come, fans from all over the world held vigil outside the Lennons' home, singing John's songs.

Instead of escaping from New York, Yoko chose the seclusion of familiar surroundings and locked herself away in the Dakota. She closed off the bedroom that she had shared with John and instructed staff to change nothing in the apartment. For three months Yoko went through severe depression, before finally admitting to herself that John would have wanted her to get on with her life. She once again took up the reins of Lennono and, more significantly, returned to the recording studio to make a new album, *Season Of Glass*: "Making the record," she later revealed, "was definitely therapy, the only way I could survive." The record's sleeve was controversial, featuring a photograph of John's bloodstained glasses, which Yoko had picked up after his shooting. Some accused her of tastelessness, although her motives were clearly deeply personal.

After all the criticism that she attracted during the early years of her relationship with John—she was, after all, popularly seen as being responsible for splitting up The Beatles— Yoko Ono at last had the world's sympathy and respect. The Dakota, where she and John shared so many traumas and triumphs, remains her home. She has continued to work as an artist, musician, and performer, often with her son Sean, now also a respected musician in his own right and signed to The Beastie Boys' hip Grand Royal label. But John Lennon still remains an important part of Yoko's life: "We were best friends but also competitive artists. To me, he is still alive. Death alone doesn't extinguish a flame and spirit like John."

After John's death, the Dakota was deluged with floral tributes from devastated Lennon fans.
Despite the trauma of her husband's death, Yoko opted to keep their apartment in the building.

Relics

John Lennon left a legacy of unfinished tracks and half-written songs and since his death a number of these have come to light. The first notable package of unreleased Lennon material, the album *Milk And Honey*, emerged in 1984. It interleaves six of John's recordings-in-progress with tracks written and recorded by Yoko. Although the versions of John's songs are unrefined, they show that he retained his caustic wit and capacity for brutal honesty. The most interesting compilation that followed John's death was simply called *Menlove Avenue*, after the street where he grew up with his Aunt Mimi. This contains out-takes from his solo albums. Many of these recordings possess a powerful raw charm—a quality missing from many of the later releases during John's lifetime.

In 1995, a modest wave of Beatlemania was unleashed. With the market for Beatle rarities and bootlegs as buoyant as ever, the *Anthology* series was conceived. A major television documentary series was accompanied by the release of three double-CD sets made up from out-takes or alternative versions of some of The Beatles' most famous songs.

In January 1994, Paul McCartney, in his capacity as one half of pop's most famous songwriting partnership, had inducted John posthumously into the Rock and Roll Hall of Fame. After the ceremony, Yoko gave Paul tapes of two of John's home demos. The idea was that with the other three Beatles playing along with John's backing track, two "new" Beatles tracks would emerge. George Martin, who played a central role in the *Anthology* series, was against the idea of the new recordings and refused to be involved. However, engineer Geoff Emerick, who had worked with The Beatles during the 1960s at Abbey Road, did lend a hand.

The first new release was "Free As A Bird," culled from two verses of an unfinished song recorded by John while improvising at the piano. Turning back the years, Paul McCartney supplied a middle-eight section. The finished song was vaguely reminiscent of *Abbey Road*-era Beatles. Another song, "Real Love," had been heard in demo form in the 1988 film of John's life, *Imagine*. Some pundits felt that producer Jeff Lynne (formerly of The Electric Light Orchestra) had simply made them sound like ELO. The remaining Beatles themselves had few qualms, though. Paul McCartney pointed out that John and he had often worked on each other's incomplete songs in the past: "It was like John bringing me a song and saying 'Do you want to finish it?'" There were both emotional and technical obstacles to overcome during the recording of the new tracks. Ringo revealed that the remaining three Beatles dealt with John's absence by pretending that he'd simply gone out for lunch, or on holiday. Both singles were worldwide hits, though neither made the top spot in the U.S. or U.K.

Sean Lennon, Yoko, and Paul McCartney gathered to honor John at the Rock and Roll Hall of Fame in 1994. Yoko and Paul embraced during the ceremony, suggesting they had finally made peace.

A man of influence

Now that the old divisions of high and low culture have largely collapsed, it is no surprise to see The Beatles respected as much as the greatest classical composers or jazz musicians. What is surprising is how much The Beatles—both as musicians and personalities—have become a part of our lives. More than 30 years since their last recordings, The Beatles remain the most famous pop group in the world. As the band's creative axis, John Lennon and Paul McCartney's influence on the course of popular music has been profound.

Most major songwriters of the past three decades would cite Lennon and McCartney as important influences, and only Bob Dylan can claim any parity in terms of cultural significance. Producers point to the collaboration between The Beatles and George Martin as a benchmark in the use of the recording studio. Every new generation throws up its own take on The Beatles. Most successful have been The Electric Light Orchestra in the 1970s and Oasis in the 1990s—indeed, the latter's *What's the Story? (Morning Glory)* achieved sales comparable to those of the Fab Four, becoming the U.K.'s second best-selling LP of all time.

Since the demise of the Fab Four, Paul McCartney has emerged as the most successful ex-Beatle in terms of record sales, and remains one of pop's best-selling artists. John Lennon idled away much of the 1970s, but retained critical respect and still took the prizes for serious artistic credibility. After all those years, he was still regarded as the "intellectual" Beatle.

Successive generations of music fans have continued to buy into the legend of The Beatles since their split. Their classic albums—especially those released between 1965's *Rubber Soul* and 1969's *Abbey Road*—continue to sell in large numbers, while John's composition "Imagine" remains one of the most popular songs of the twentieth century.

Some would claim John Lennon was a genius. He himself was characteristically unfazed by the tag, once stating: "If there is such a thing as a genius, I am one. If there isn't, I don't care." Lennon was certainly full of contradictions. While he was capable of exhibiting a hard exterior, those who got close to him spoke of his kindness, and generosity. But while he was capable of acts of cruelty and extreme selfishness, John also publicly stood up for the most positive aspects of humanity. He preached the very spirit of his age—love, peace, and understanding—as vociferously, even belligerently, as anyone.

When asked at the height of Beatlemania how long he thought the Beatles would last, John Lennon's reply was a cautious one: "You can be big-headed and say 'Yeah, we're gonna last 10 years,' but as soon as you've said that you think … we're lucky if we last three months." It's now over 40 years since his school band, The Quarrymen, played their first ramshackle skiffle concerts, but the legacy of John Lennon will shine on for decades to come.

John Lennon photographed in 1971. An icon of his time, and one of the best smiles in pop.

Index